T0355060

ENGLISH
FOR UNIVERSITY
ASPIRANTS
WORKBOOK

FRANCIS A. ANDREW

www.trafford.com
North America & international
toll-free: 844-688-6899 (USA & Canada)
fax: 812 355 4082

CONTENTS

THEME 1

VARIOUS

UNIT 1
Now and Then

_1_____2_____3_____4_____5_____6_____

Omar spoke his first word   He started school

___7_____8_____9_____10_____11_____12

He started to learn English   He learned judo   He went to the USA

_13____14_____15_____16_____17_____18___

    He passed the school exams   He went to high School   He got to university

Omar is now 19 years old.

Using the simple past tense, look at the time line and answer the questions about Omar.

Example: How many years ago did he speak his first word?

He spoke his first word 17 years ago.

1.) How old was Omar when he started school?

_____

_____.

2.) How many years ago did Omar start to learn English?

_____

_____.

3.) How long ago did Omar learn judo?

_____

_____.

4.) Where did Omar go when he was 11 years old?

_____

_____.

5.) What did Omar pass when he was 14 years old?

_____

_____.

6.) Which school did he go to when he was 16 years old?

_____

_____.

7.) When did he get into university?

_____

_____.

Answer the following questions using either the present simple or the past simple

1.) What year is it now?

_____

2.) What month is it now?

_____

3.) What day is it today?

_____

4.) What time do you usually get up?

_____

5.) Where do you always watch television?

_____

6.) How old were you when you started to learn English?

_____

7.) When did you last drink some tea?

_____

8.) How old were you when you first ate halwa?

_____

9.) What did you see on television yesterday?

_____

10.) When did you last play a computer game?

_____

Change these sentences into the negative past simple

Example: I played football last Saturday.

I didn't play football last Saturday.

1.) I watched television for three hours yesterday.

_____

2.) I ate a big lunch today.

_____

3.) My brother caught a big fish last week.

_____

4.) My family and I went to Australia last February.

_____

5.) Ahmed drank five cups of tea.

_____

6.) Manchester United scored three goals in their match against Liverpool.

_____

7.) Our team came first in the competition.

_____

8.) Tom won a gold medal in the race.

_____

9.) My sister cooked the dinner last night.

_____

10.) They saw the accident.

_____

Change these negative sentences into the affirmative past simple

Example: I didn't play football last Thursday.

I played football last Thursday.

1.) Father didn't wash the car last week.

_____

2.) My little brother didn't do his homework yesterday.

_____

3.) We didn't understand the maths lesson.

_____

4.) John didn't know where to go.

_____

5.) The supermarket didn't open at 8.30 am.

_____

6.) It didn't rain yesterday evening.

_____

7.) The shop didn't close at 5.30pm

_____

8.) We didn't buy bread this morning.

_____

9.) Amar didn't sell his old car.

_____

10.) The mechanic didn't repair the bus.

_____

Put a circle around the correct word in _italics._

My name _is / are_ Fatma. I _am / are_ a schoolgirl. Every day I _went / go_ to a school in Muscat. I _learn / learns_ many subjects at school – English, Geography, Mathematics, French, Physics, Chemistry and Biology. _Me / My_ teachers _are / is_ very good. I _liked / like_ my school very much. My friends and I _enjoy / enjoy_ed going to this school. We are very lucky. Now I _are / am_ 16 years _olds / old._

However, when my grandparents _was / were_ my age, they _were / was_ not so lucky. They _didn't / don't_ go to school when they _was / were_ children. They _learn / learned_ to read and write from their parents. A teacher in their village _taught / teach_ them how to count. My grandfather _take care of / took care of_ camels and my grandmother _help / helped_ her mother in the house.

Put the words in the correct order

Example: cleaned car father my yesterday the

      My father cleaned the car yesterday.

1.) to office day every I my go

_____

2.) swam in we sea the Sunday on

_____

3.) cousin job oil week rig my an last a got on

_____

4.) cake mother our a made

_____

5.) likes beach go Ahmed to summer in the to the

_____

UNIT 2
Your health and well-being

toothache, a stomachache, a cold, earache, a temperature, a headache,

Use the above words to complete the sentences.

1.) I feel very hot. I have _____

2.) Ahmed has pain in his teeth. He has _____

3.) Ali and Saleh are sneezing a lot. They have _____

4.) You have a pain in your stomach. You have _____

5.) We have pain in our ears. We have _____

6.) Noor has pain in her head. She has _____

Rewrite the following sentences using contractions.

Example: Basem has got a cold.

Basem's got a cold

1.) I have got the mumps.

_____

2.) Dafiya has got the measles.

_____

3.) We have got whooping cough.

_____

4.) They have got influenza.

_____

5.) Johnny cannot get out of bed.

_____

6.) Johnny is sick.

_____

7.) They are sick.

_____

8.) I am much better now.

_____

9.) You are going to see the doctor.

_____

10.) The doctor is going to prescribe you some medicine.

_____

Give advice to these people with these medical conditions. Using the modal verb *should* write two sentences – one affirmative and the other negative.

Example: A man who is very fat. (eat less / eat so much)

You should eat less. You shouldn't eat so much.

1.) A lazy boy who never does exercise and who watches a lot of television. (exercise more / watch television such a lot)

_____

_____.

2.) Someone who crosses the street without looking. (more careful crossing the street / cross street without looking)

_____

_____.

3.) A man who eats a lot of cakes but never eats fruit and vegetables. (eat more fruit and vegetables / eat so many cakes)

_____

_____.

4.) A boy with an injured leg who wants to play football. (play football with an injured leg / wait until your leg has healed)

_____

_____.

5.) A man who smokes forty cigarettes a day. (smoke so many cigarettes / stop smoking)

_____

_____.

FRANCIS A. ANDREW

Choose from the following list the opposite to each of the ten adjectives listed below.

healthy, worse, fast, infectious, open, cold, up, sad, in, noisy,

1.) quiet _____

2.) non-infectious _____

3.) down _____

4.) slow_____

5.) sick_____

6.) closed_____

7.) better_____

8.) hot_____

9.) out_____

10.)happy_____

Make questions for these sentences using the "Wh" words. Choose from the following list.

Example: I am going to the clinic.

Where are you going?

Who, Where, When Why, Whose, How many, How, What, Which, What time

1.) I have got a very sore throat.

_____?_

2.) They went to the hospital.

_____ _____?_

3.) We saw the specialist at 4 o'clock.

_____ __ _____?_

4.) John will have an operation next week.

_____?_

5.) He will have his operation in the Central Hospital.

_____?_

6.) You see the nurse regularly.

_____?_

7.) I stayed at home because I was feeling unwell.

_____?_

8.) That is Dr. Ahmed's office.

_____?_

9.) They took the accident victims to the hospital by ambulance.

_____?_

10.) There are 20 patients waiting to see the doctor.

_____?_

Read the passage and say if the following sentences are true (T) or false (F)

It is important to eat a varied diet if you want to keep healthy. You should eat lots of vegetables and fruit. You should eat fish often but not too much red meat like mutton and beef. Chicken is very good for you too. It is necessary to drink a lot of water especially in the hot weather. You should avoid smoking. It is a good idea to do plenty of exercise. Going to the gym three times a week is a good habit to get into. And it is vital to get plenty of sleep. You should not go to bed later than 10 O'clock.

1.) You should eat a variety of foods. _____

2.) Vegetables and fruit are unimportant. _____

3.) For a healthy diet you should eat a large amount of mutton and beef. _____

4.) Chicken is a healthy food. _____

5.) You should avoid drinking water in the summer. _____

6.) Smoking is healthy. _____

7.) Exercise is unimportant. _____

8.) Going to the gym is not a good routine. _____

9.) Getting plenty of sleep is important. _____

10.) It is alright to go to bed after ten o'clock. _____

UNIT 3
Animals in Oman

Not many people have seen an Arabian Leopard but those who have seen it say that it is an amazing animal. Sadly, only 200 of these animals now live in the mountains of Dhofar – they are now on the danger list. These beautiful animals are almost extinct.

The ray-finned fish lives in the mountains of northern Oman. However, it can also be discovered in parts of the UAE. One species of the Oman Garra is blind, and lives in underground caves. They are blind because they live in places where there is no light.

The Arabian Oryx isn't exclusive to Oman, it lives in other countries too. Its natural habitat is in the deserts of Muscat and Dhofar. It's also the national animal of The Sultanate of Oman, UAE, Qatar, Jordan, and Bahrain. This animal was endangered but its numbers are now increasing. You can see the oryx at the Arabian Oryx Sanctuary in the Governorate of Al Wusta,

What do the words mean? Choose from the following list.

special, wonderful, becoming more, cannot see, a place where an animal lives, in danger of disappearing, a type of animal, an animal that does not exist now, found, a safe place

1.) amazing _____

2.) extinct _____

3.) discovered _____

4.) blind _____

5.) species _____

6.) exclusive _____

7.) natural habitat _____

8.) endangered _____

9.) increasing _____

10.) sanctuary _____

Look at the following text and put a circle around the correct word (s) from the words in *italics*.

Last week Ahmed and his family *visit / visited* the zoo. They *saw / see* lots of animals there. Ali and Hassan, Ahmed's two sons, *like / liked* the monkeys. The monkeys *were swinging / was swinging* from the trees. "Let's *go / goes* and see the Arabian Leopard," said Ali. "Why *does you want / do you want* to see the Arabian Leopard," Hassan asked his brother. "Because it is an *endanger / endangered* species," replied Ali. "Ali is right," said Noora their mother. "Maybe this *will / will be* the last time you will see one. "They might become *extinct / extinction* in the mountains," said Ahmed, but they *will be / will been* safe in zoos and sanctuaries.

Say what these people and animals do. Choose from the following list.

grows vegetables and raises animals,   is where there are lots of trees,   catches mice,   eats grass,   catches fish,   you can see lots of animals,   spoils nature,   looks for animals and kills them,   illegally kills animals,   lives in the desert,

1.) a farmer _____

2.) a hunter _____

3.) a fisherman _____

4.) a cat _____

5.) the oryx _____

6.) in a zoo _____

7.) a horse _____

8.) a polluter _____

9.) a poacher _____

10.) a forest

Put the words in *italics* into the past simple.

I *don't kill* _____animals during my last holiday. My friends and I *gp* _____to a

nature reserve in Bahrain. We *help* _____
the zoologists to take care of the animals there. Jasim, Ali,
Othman and I *feed* _____the oryxes
there. We *spend* _____a week in
Bahrain. Then we *return*_____ to Oman.
When we *come* _____back to Oman, we *go*
_____to Qurum Beach. Then we *clean*
_____up the beach. Some people throw their
rubbish on the sand. My friends and I and some other volunteers,
pick _____up the rubbish. The
beach *is* _____nice and clean when we
*finish*_____.

Read the following paragraph

There is a kind of medicine used in Oman; it is called traditional
medicine – sometimes it is called ethnomedicine. Special doctors,
called traditional healers know how to use special plants to treat
minor illnesses like colds, fevers, headaches, stomachaches and
influenza.

Lime, honey and garlic are used to treat throat infections,
diabetes and obesity. Cinnamon is used to treat throat infections.
Frankincense, from the frankincense trees in Salalah is used to cure
stomach disorders.

There are about 33 plants in Oman that are used in ethnomedicine.
Maybe researchers will discover more plants that can help cure
sicknesses.

**Correct the following sentences using negative and affirmative
sentences.**

Example: Traditional medicine and ethnomedicne are different.

Traditional medicine and ethnomedicine are not different.
Traditional medicine and ethnomedicine are the same.

FRANCIS A. ANDREW

1.) Traditional healers use pharmaceutical medicines to treat minor illnesses.

_____

_____

_____

2.) Colds, fevers, headaches, stomachaches and influenza are major illnesses.

_____

_____

_____

3.) Lime, garlic and honey are used to treat headaches and stomachaches.

_____

_____

_____

4.) Cinnamon is used to treat cancer.

_____

_____

_____

5.) Frankincense comes from the frankincense trees in Sur.

_____

_____

_____

16

6.) There are forty-three plants in Oman that are used in ethnomedicine.

_____

_____

_____

Rewrite the sentences changing the verbs in _italics_ into the present perfect tense.

Example: I *opened* the door.

I have opened the door.

1.) The doctor *gave* Maria some medicine.

_____

2.) Maria *took* the medicine.

_____

3.) The students *did* their exam.

_____

4.) I *cleaned* the car.

_____

5.) The surgeon *operated* on the patient.

_____

6.) Omar and his family *went* to the zoo.

_____

7.) They *saw* many interesting animals there.

_____

8.) You *read* your book.

_____

9.) My sister *bought* a kitten.

_____

10.) My brother and I *ate* a pizza.

_____

UNIT 4
Celebrations in Oman

A traditional Oman wedding is very interesting. The Mulkah is a ceremony at the mosque. The bridegroom attends the Mulkah with his male relatives and friends. After this ceremony the couple are married. The women are with the bride. During this time, they eat and celebrate. The bridegroom then arrives in a caravan of cars and takes his bride back to his house. It is a happy occasion. Everyone has a good time.

What do the words mean? Choose from the following list.

a line of vehicles,   family members,   something which people have done for a long time,   when something special happens, the man who will be the husband,   actions which are performed for something important,   happy activities because something good has happened,   the husband and wife,   the woman who will be the wife,   all people

1.) traditional _____

2.) bridegroom _____

3.) bride _____

4.) ceremony _____

5.) couple _____

6.) celebrate _____

7.) caravan _____

8.) relatives _____

9.) occasion _____

10.) everyone _____

Read the following passage

The Muscat Festival is one of the most important festivals in Oman. The festival shows the industrial and technological development of Oman but also how Oman has preserved its culture and traditions. The festival is usually in January and February of each year. It provides a great opportunity for sightseeing and shopping. Peter Jones, a tourist from America is talking to his friend Omran about a day he had at the Muscat Festival.

Omran: So how did you like the Muscat Festival, Peter?

Peter: It was really interesting. I bought a traditional Omani dishdasha.

Omran: What else did you see at the festival?

Peter: I saw some theatre performances. The Omani actors and actresses were wearing traditional Omani costumes. I also saw some acrobatic events. It was amazing to see the athletes jumping high and doing somersaults when they were in the air.

Omran: Did you see the camel races?

Peter: Yes I did. I didn't know camels could run so fast.

Omran: Well, Peter, I'm glad you enjoyed the festival.

Peter: But I am going to go again tomorrow. I didn't see everything.

Omran: You are right, Peter. You need a few days to have a real experience of the Muscat Festival.

Peter: Great. I will go again tomorrow – and the day after tomorrow.

Answer the following questions in complete sentences

1.) What is one of the most important festivals in Oman?

_____

_____

2.) When can you see the festival?

_____

_____

3.) Who is Peter Jones?

_____

_____

4.) Who is he talking to?

_____

_____

5.) What did Peter buy at the Festival?

_____

_____

6.) What were the Omani actors and actresses wearing?

_____

_____

7.) What didn't Peter know about camels?

_____

_____

8.) When will Peter go to the Festival again?

_____

_____

9.) How many days do you need to have a real experience of the Muscat Festival?

_____

_____

10.) How many more days will Peter spend at the Muscat Festival?

_____

_____

Underline the best definition of the following words. Choose from the definitions in *italics*.

1.) Preserve: *to keep something in good condition and stop it from being destroyed / to throw something away because you don't want it*

2.) Opportunity: *buying something / a good chance*

3.) Provide: *to take away / to give*

4.) Sightseeing: *looking at interesting things when you are on holiday / getting your eyes tested for new glasses*

5.) Tourist: *a businessman / a person who is on holiday in another country*

6.) Amazing: *boring / very interesting*

7.) Glad: *pleased / sad*

8.) Athletes: *actors and actresses / sportsmen and sportswomen*

9.) A few: *some / many*

10.) The day after tomorrow: *the next day / in two days*

Rewrite the following sentences with the correct punctuation.

Example: go salalah year i every to the festival

I go to the Salalah Festival every year.

1.) festival the between and june year september salalah place takes every

_____

_____

2.) good is climate salalah summer the of the in

_____

_____

3.) interesting festival everyone for the has something

_____

_____

4.) 2019 festival july 11th in the began on

_____

_____

5.) people were at festival the some signing

_____

_____

6.) festival tourism salalah helps increase the in

_____

_____

7.) omani you at eat festival can food traditional the

_____

_____

8.) are performers salalah at festival there theatre the

_____

_____

9.) buy people kebabs festival at can shwarmas the and

_____

_____

10.) amazing see can acrobatics the at festival you

_____

_____

Change the verb in brackets into the correct tense according to the time expression

Example: My friends and I (go) to Muscat next week

My friends and I will go to Muscat next week.

1.) My friends and I (go) to the Sultan Camel Race two months ago.

_____

_____

2.) The camels (compete) on a racetrack when we were there.

_____

_____

3.) Camels always (run) very fast.

_____

_____

4.) Omanis (race) camels for centuries.

_____

_____

5.) Last week we (see) a camel running at 64 kilometers an hour.

_____

_____

6.) My friend Khalid (have) ten camels.

_____

_____

7.) He (have) camels since he was twelve years old.

_____

_____

8.) Camels with one hump (call) dromedaries.

_____

_____

9.) I (buy) a camel yesterday.

_____

_____

10.) Jasim's camel (be) the fastest in the last Sultan Camel Race Cup.

_____

_____

Rearrange the letters to make words.

Example: **esrho** A very fast animal often used in racing
_____horse_____

1.) **lacem** An animal that you use for traveling in the desert

_____

2.) **ydbrihta** You celebrate this when you are one year older

_____

3.) **afevsitl** Every year there is one in Muscat and one in Salalah

_____

4.) **ide** This comes after Ramadan _____

5.) **ecletaerb** You do this when you are happy and successful

_____

6.) **wahla** You eat this on special occasions _____

7.) **newdigd** A ceremony when people get married_____

8.) **onacsoci** When something special happens_____

9.) **soidtntiar** Thigs which people have always done and still do _____

10.)**ecra** When people or animals are running and trying to win _____

UNIT 5
The Future

Life in the future will be very different to what it is today. Maha and her friend Afra are talking about how things might be different fifty years from now.

Maha: The world is going to be a very different place fifty years from now, Afra.

Afra: Yes it is. I have often thought about how exactly it will be different. The way we live and do things aren't going to be the same.

Maha: I think that planes will be supersonic. We will be able to fly from Muscat to New York in only two hours.

Maha: Education will be different. I think robots will teach us.

Afra: Really? Do you think there will be no human teachers?

Maha: There will be some but they will not be as important as the robots.

Afra: And we are going to have more leisure time.

Maha: Why do you think that?

Afra: Because robots will be doing most of the work – especially in factories.

Maha: I think a lot of people are going to be living in houses on the sea and under the sea.

Afra: I think so too. There won't be enough land to build houses for all the people of the world.

Maha: And we are going to have to grow more of our food under the sea.

Afra: Yes. There isn't going to be enough farmland to grow food to feed a much bigger population.

Maha: In fifty years from now, most of the fish we eat will come from fish farms.

Afra: Yes. We are taking too many fish from the sea. Some fish species could become extinct.

Correct the following sentences. Use a negative and an affirmative sentence.

Example: Maha and Afra are talking about life forty years from now.

They aren't talking about life forty years from now. They are talking about life fifty years from now.

    1.) Afra has often thought about how the world will be the same.

    _____

    _____

    _____

2.) Maha thinks we will be able to fly from Muscat to New York in six hours.

_____

_____

_____

3.) Maha thinks that teachers will be more important than robots.

_____

_____

_____

4.) Afra says we are going to have less leisure time?

_____

_____

_____

5.) Afra tells Maha that people will do most of the work in factories.

_____

_____

_____

6.) Maha says a lot of people are going to be living in houses on the land.

_____

_____

_____

7.) Maha tells Afra that we are going to grow more of our food on farmland.

_____

_____

_____

8.) In the next fifty years, world population will decrease.

_____

_____

_____

9.) Maha predicts that in fifty years from now, most of the fish we eat will be caught in the sea.

_____

_____

_____

10.) Afra says we are taking too little fish from the sea.

_____

_____

_____

Change the verbs in _italics_ into the future tense. Use both the "will" and "going to" forms.

I will go to the supermarket now.

We _are drinking_ some tea.
We are going to drink some tea.

1.) Our class *visit* the Natural History Museum in London.

_____

_____

2.) We *are seeing* the dinosaurs and other extinct animals.

_____

_____

3.) Some scientists *make* predictions on climate change.

_____

_____

4.) There are architects who *are planning* the cities of the future.

_____

_____

5.) Zoologists at Edinburgh University *are doing* experiments with human and animal DNA.

_____

_____

6.) They *create* new species of animals by genetic modification.

_____

_____

7.) Botanists *are perform* the same kind of experiments with plants.

_____

_____

8.) Ahmed Ali is studying Biology at University. He *is being* a biologist

_____

_____

9.) Jasim Mohammed *start* his own business.

_____

_____

10.) He *is selling* machines to factories.

_____

_____

What do the words mean? Choose from the following list.

a building where you can see old things, a scientist who studies animals, moves faster than the speed of sound, someone who draws plans for buildings, a machine that looks and acts like a human, free time, an animals that does not exist now, a scientist who studies plants, do something, make something, a farm for breeding fish, altering the genes of a plant of animal, say what you think will happen in the future, type of animal or plant, do something in the laboratory to see what the result is

1.) supersonic _____

2.) predict _____

3.) robot _____

4.) perform _____

5.) leisure _____

6.) fish farm _____

7.) species _____

8.) dinosaur _____

9.) museum _____

10.) zoologist _____

11.) botanist _____

12.) experiment _____

13.) genetic modification _____

14.) create _____

15.) architect _____

Read the following passage.

We have no idea what computers will be like in 2030 because change is happening so quickly. We know that quantum computing – the introduction of physics into the field of computer science – is going to be extremely important. Computers are going to become really, very tiny, the size of an atom. That's going to make a huge difference. Nano-computing, very small computers that you might swallow inside a pill will then learn about your illness and start curing it. That brings together biological computing as well, where we can print parts of the body. So I think we're going to see computers coming into all aspects of our lives. We must hope that the changes we will see in computer science will be the benefit of humanity. Computers must be our servants and not our masters.

Say if the following are true (T) or false (F)

1.) We know exactly what computers will be like in 2030.
_____

2.) Change is happening very slowly. _____

3.) It is important to connect physics with computing. _____

4.) Nano-computing means very large computers. _____

5.) Computers the size of atoms could be put in medicines

_____

6.) In future, we might be able to print parts of the body.

_____

7.) We will not see computers in every aspect of our lives.

_____

8.) We hope that computers in future help human beings.

_____

9.) Computers must be our bosses. _____

10.) We must serve computers in the future. _____

Correct the spelling mistakes in the following paragraph. Rewrite the passage using the correct spelling.

I am eihgt years old. My grandfather told me that when he was mye age he didn't have a compoter. There wuz no internit, so when he wanted to get infurmashion, he went to the libray and got it from boks. And he only had a blak and wite televishion with tow channels. There was no e-mal when he was a boy. People rote lettrs to each other.

_____

_____

_____

_____

_____

FRANCIS A. ANDREW

_____

_____

_____

_____

_____

_____

Rewrite the following paragraph putting the verbs in *italics* into the correct tense.

I *is going to buy* a new car next week. My family and I *am going to drive* to Salalah in it. I *will no* drive all the way. My brother *are going to come* with us, and he *will drives* half of the way there. We *am going to do* sightseeing in Salalah. We *will staying* in Salalah for two weeks. We *isn't going to stay* for three weeks.

_____

_____

_____

_____

_____

_____

_____

_____

_____

THEME 2

CIVILISATIONS

UNIT 1
Nebraska Man

In 1922, solely on the basis of a worn fossil tooth from Nebraska, paleontologist Henry Fairfield Osborn described *Hesperopithecus haroldcookii* as the first anthropoid ape from North America. Five years later, Osborn's colleague William King Gregory concluded that the tooth most likely came from an extinct, a pig-like animal.

For five years, many people thought that this was a new discovery that was made. Like Piltdown man you read about in the student's book, Nebraska man turned out to be fake.

What do these words and phrases mean? Choose from the following list.

finally say,   only,   species no longer in existence,   animals that resemble humans / walk on their hind legs,   prove to be, damaged and shabby as the result of much use,   someone you work with

1. solely

2. worn

3. anthropoid ape

4. colleague

5. conclude

6. turn out

7. extinct

1. **Project:**
   Go on the internet or read some books on an extinct species of plant or animal. Do not use the dinosaurs. Write about 150 words.

2. Find out from the internet or books, something like Piltdown Man. A fossil which tuned out to be a fake. Write about 150 words.

UNIT 2
Ancient Civilisations

For almost 30 centuries—from its unification around 3100 B.C. to its conquest by Alexander the Great in 332 B.C.—ancient Egypt was the preeminent civilization in the Mediterranean world. From the great pyramids of the Old Kingdom through the military conquests of the New Kingdom, Egypt's greatness has long entranced archaeologists and historians and created a vibrant field of study all its own: Egyptology. The main sources of information about ancient Egypt are the many monuments, objects and artefacts that have been recovered from archaeological sites, covered with hieroglyphs that have only recently been deciphered.

What do these words and phrases mean? Choose from the following list.

energetic,   better than all others,   filled with wonder and delight,   succeed in understanding,   made into one whole, retrieve,   a writing system using pictures,   an object of cultural interest,   a structure built to commemorate a notable person or event,   to defeat a country or people in war

1. unification

2. conquest

3. preeminent

4. entrance

5. vibrant

6. monument

7. artefacts

8. recover

9. hieroglyphs

10. decipher

Project 1. Go on the internet and find out what you can about an ancient civilisation. Write about 150 words.

Project 2. Go on the internet and find out what artefacts have been recovered from another ancient civilisation. Write about 100 words.

UNIT 3
The Romans in Spain

The Romans first came to Spain in 206 BC when they invaded the Iberian Peninsula from the south. They fought the Iberians and defeated them at Alcalá del Rio, which is near today's Seville. On this site the town of Itálica was founded and Spain fell under Roman occupation for the next 700 years. In the north, however, the Celts and Basques continued to fight the Romans and didn't fall until 19 BC. In all it took the Romans two centuries to gain complete control of Spain.

What do these words and phrases mean? Choose from the following list.

100 years,   beat,   *take part in a violent struggle involving the exchange of physical blows or the use of weapons,   to be captured or defeated,   a place,   to be subject to, established*

1. defeat

2. site

3. founded

4. fight / fought

5. fell under

6. fall

7. century

Project. The Romans conquered much of Europe. You have read about how they conquered Britain (student's book) and how they conquered Spain (workbook). Go on the internet and write about one other place they conquered. Write approximately 200 words.

UNIT 4
The Greeks

The classical period was an era of war and conflict—first between the Greeks and the Persians, then between the Athenians and the Spartans—but it was also an era of unprecedented political and cultural achievement. Besides the Parthenon and Greek tragedy, classical Greece brought us the historian Herodotus, the physician Hippocrates and the philosopher Socrates.

What do the following words and phrases mean? Choose from the following list.

a medical doctor, a period in history, concerning government administration, one who studies the nature of reality, never done or known before, an event which causes great suffering

1. era

2. unprecedented

3. political

4. tragedy

5. physician

6. philosopher

Project 1. The Greeks conquered a lot of territories. Choose one of the places they conquered and write about how that conquered it. Write about 150 words.

Project 2. Alexander the Great conquered many territories for the Greeks. Find out about him. Write about 150 words.

THEME 3

STORIES

UNIT 1
Goldilocks and the Three Bears

Once upon a time, there was a little girl named Goldilocks. She went for a walk in the forest. Pretty soon, she came upon a house. She knocked and, when no one answered, she walked right in.

What do these words and phrases mean? Choose from the following list.

to strike something with the knuckles,   at one time in the past, quite soon,   to find something by chance,   thousands of trees all clustered together

1. once upon a time

2. forest

3. come upon

4. knock

5. pretty soon

Project 1. Tell the full story of Goldilocks in your own words.

Project 2. Do you know a fairy story from Oman involving animals? Write about it in your own words.

UNIT 2
Little Red Riding Hood

Once upon a time there lived a little country girl, the prettiest creature who was ever seen. Her mother had a little red riding hood made for her. Everybody called her Little Red Riding Hood.

One day her mother said to her: "Go my dear, and see how your grandmother is doing, for I hear she has been very ill."

Little Red Riding Hood set out immediately.

As she was going through the wood, she met with a wolf. He asked her where she was going.

What do these words and phrases mean? Choose from the following list.

most beautiful,   outside a city or a town,   dangerous dog-like animal,   a covering for the head and neck,   a lot of trees together – but smaller than a forest

1. the country

2. prettiest

3. hood

4. woods

5. wolf

Project 1. Can you tell the story of Little Red Riding Hood? Write about it in your own words.

Project 2. Do you know a fairy story from Oman that involves a dangerous animal? Write about it in your own words.

UNIT 3
Cinderella

ONCE UPON A TIME a girl named Cinderella lived with her stepmother and two stepsisters. Poor Cinderella had to work hard all day long so the others could rest. It was she who had to wake up each morning when it was still dark and cold to start the fire. It was she who cooked the meals. It was she who kept the fire going. The poor girl could not stay clean, from all the ashes and cinders by the fire.

What do these words and phrases mean? Choose from the following list.

the powdery residue left after the burning of a substance, a small piece of partly burnt coal or wood

1. ashes

2. cinder

Project 1. Can you tell the full story of Cinderella in your own words?

Project 2. Do you know any story from Oman that involves a magical piece of clothing ?

UNIT 4
The Sleeping Beauty

Once upon a time, there lived a king and a queen, who had no children. They were so sorry about having no children, that I cannot tell you how sorry they were. At last, however, after many years, the queen had a daughter.

There was a very fine christening for the baby princess. The king and queen looked throughout the kingdom for fairies to be her sponsors, and they found seven fairies. Each fairy sponsor was to give the princess a gift, as was the custom of fairies in those days. In this way, the princess had all the perfections imaginable.

What do these words and phrases mean? Choose from the following list.

a present, the male ruler of a state, the one who vouches for the child at its christening, the female ruler of a state, a tradition, the daughter of a king and queen, something that

happens eventually after a long wait,   without spot or blemish,
that can be imagined,   the naming ceremony of a child

1. king

2. queen

3. at last

4. christening

5. princess

6. sponsor

7. gift

8. perfections

9. imaginable

10. custom

Project 1. Can you tell the story of the sleeping beauty in your own words?

Project 2. Are there any fairy stories from Oman which have wicked fairies in them? Tell one of these stories in your own words.

THEME 4

MARTIAL ARTS

UNIT 1
Jiu Jitsu

Brazilian Jiu-Jitsu is a martial art and combat sport based on ground fighting and submission holds. It focuses on the skill of taking an opponent to the ground, controlling one's opponent, gaining a dominant position, and using a number of techniques to force them into submission via joint locks or chokeholds.

What do these words and phrases mean? Choose from the following list.

surrender / give up, *hold which involves encircling the neck of another,* *putting your opponent in a position where he cannot move*

1. lock

2. chokeholds

3. submission

Project: Go on the internet and find out how popular jiu jitsu is in Oman. Write about 100 words.

UNIT 2
Muay Thai

Muay Thai, sometimes referred to as "Thai boxing," is a martial art and combat sport that uses stand-up striking along with various clinching techniques. This discipline is known as the "art of eight limbs," as it is characterised by the combined use of fists, elbows, knees, and shins.

What do these words and phrases mean? Choose from the following list.

an arm or a leg,   the larger bones on the lower leg,   grapple very closely,   describe the distinctive nature or features of something,   joint between the upper and lower leg,   join

1. clinching

2. limb

3. characterise

4. combine

5. knee

6. shin

Project: Find out as much as you can about Muay Thai. How widespread is it in Oman? Write about 100 words.

UNIT 3
Mixed Martial Arts (MMA)

Mixed martial arts, sometimes referred to as cage fighting, no holds barred, and ultimate fighting, is a full-contact combat sport based on striking, grappling and ground fighting, incorporating techniques from various combat sports including boxing, kickboxing and martial arts from around the world.

What do these words mean? Choose from the following list.

the best or most extreme example,   to take in / combine, forbidden / not allowed

1. barred

2. incorporate

3. ultimate

Project: Is MMA practiced a lot in Oman? Find out by going on the internet.

UNIT 4
Martial Arts and you.

Project: Have you ever practised a martial art? If so, which one? Or
If you haven't, which one would like to take up.

THEME 5

NATURAL DISASTERS AND ADVERSE WEATHER CONDITIONS

UNIT 1
Heavy rain

Torrential rains that battered <u>Oman</u> are bringing waterfalls back to the country, turning parched valleys into flowing water parks.

<u>Rain that reached 120 millimetres in some areas</u> is creating waterfalls that are pulling in domestic tourists. The wet weather is a boon for some farmers whose irrigation systems are benefiting.

What do these words and phrases mean? Choose from the following list.

movement of a liquid – especially water, extremely heavy rains, the artificial application of water to soil, harmful, a river or other body of water's steep fall over a rocky ledge into a plunge pool below, strike repeatedly with hard blows, an advantage, tourists who are of the same country, a thing that is helpful

1. torrential rains

2. batter

3. flow

4. waterfall

5. domestic tourists

6. boon

7. irrigation

8. benefit

9. detrimental

Project 1. Find out how rain benefits some farmers. Write about 100 words.

Project 2. Find out how rain is detrimental to some farmers, Write about 100 words.

UNIT 2
Heavy snow

A winter storm is a combination of heavy snow, blowing snow and/ or dangerous wind chills. A winter storm is life-threatening.

Blizzards are dangerous winter storms that are a combination of blowing snow and wind resulting in very low visibilities. While heavy snowfalls and severe cold often accompany blizzards, they are not required. Sometimes strong winds pick up snow that has already fallen, creating a ground blizzard.

What do these words and phrases mean? Choose from the following list.

go with,   an unpleasant feeling of cold,   something that may kill you,   very great / intense

1. chill

2. life-threatening

3. severe

4. accompany

Project, Where does it snow in Oman? Write about it. 100 words.

UNIT 3
Storms at Sea

I have gone thrice to Antarctica sailed twice from India to Antarctica by ships. Once from South Africa to Antarctica by ship.

Antarctica is surrounded by the stormiest oceans in the world and therefore, one has to face a cyclone irrespective of your desires.

What do these words mean? Choose from the following list.

three times,   what you greatly want,   continent of ice near the south pole,   regardless,   a storm rotating counter-clockwise

1. thrice

2. Antarctica

3. cyclone

4. irrespective

5. desire

Project. Go on the internet. Find out about a storm at sea. Write about 150 words about it.

UNIT 4
You and an adverse weather condition.

Project. Choose any adverse weather condition that is mentioned in the student's book or workbook (or from any other source) that affected you. Describe how you dealt with it. Write about 150 words.

THEME 6

PALACES

UNIT 1
Kensington Palace

Kensington Palace, a palace of secret stories and public lives, has been influenced by generations of royal women.

Experience life as an 18th-century royal courtier whilst making your way through the magnificent King's and Queen's State Apartments adorned with remarkable paintings from the Royal Collection.

Victoria Revealed, set within the rooms Queen Victoria lived in as a child, is an exhibition that explores her life and reign as wife, mother, Queen and Empress.

What do these words and phrases mean? Choose from the following list.

a person who attends a royal court as a companion or adviser to the king or queen,   a public display of items of interest, having the status of a king or queen or a member of their family, fantastic / grand,   the female ruler of an empire,   the knowledge or skill acquired over a period

1. royal

2. experience

3. courtier

4. magnificent

5. exhibition

6. Empress

Project 1: Find out as much as you can about Kensington Palace. Write about 150 words.

Project 2: Choose a palace in Britain and write about it. Write about 150 words.

UNIT 2
Palace of Fontainebleau

Originally built during the 12th century, the Château de Fontainebleau was extended, renovated and improved by many kings, an emperor and a president throughout its long history. Located in the city of Fontainebleau and surrounded by a large forest of the same name, the 1,500 rooms it contains make it one of the largest castles in France. It was among the favourite residences of Napoléon, and you can see his throne and crown in the former king's chamber. You should take the very informative audio guide available during your visit, to learn more about the historical importance of this castle.

What do these words and phrases mean? Choose from the following list.

the male ruler of an empire,   a private room – especially a bedroom,   a place to live,   to restore a building,   the previous one,   what a king or a queen sits on,   what a king or a queen wear on his/her head

1. renovate

2. emperor

3. residence

4. throne

5. crown

6. former

7. chamber

Project 1: Find out as much as you can about Fontainebleau Palace. Write about 150 words.

Project 2: Choose a palace in France and write about it. Write about 150 words.

UNIT 3
Jabreen Castle

Built by Imam Bel'arab bin Sultan Al Yarubi, the 17th century Jabreen Castle rises majestically from the desert plains at the foot of the Akhdar mountain range. One of Oman's best-preserved historic buildings, the grandiose castle flawlessly retains its original spirit. Thick, pink-tinged sandstone walls give way to elegant arches, framed by the undulating line of battlements. Unlike many of Oman's forts the palatial residence wasn't built for defence purposes, so its interior is strikingly ornamented. Elegant chambers feature intricately hand-painted ceilings while arches are inscribed with Arabian calligraphy. It was Imam Bel'arab bin Sultan Al Yarubi's passion for science and art that led to Jabreen Castle becoming the most beautiful historic sites in Oman.

What do these words and phrases mean? Choose from the following list.

at the bottom of something, slightly colour, decorative handwriting, without fault, showing impressive beauty, sedimentary rock, maintain, writing or carving words on something, handsome, impressive and imposing in appearance, attracting attention, the regularly spaced openings at the top of a castle, very complicated, smooth up and down motion

1. majestic

2. foot

3. preserve

4. grandiose

5. flawless

6. tinged

7. sandstone

8. elegant

9. undulating

10. battlements

11. striking

12. intricate

13. inscribe

14. calligraphy

Project 1: Find out as much as you can about Jabreen Castle. Write about 150 words.

Project 2: Choose a palace, fort, or castle in Oman and write about it. Write about 150 words.

UNIT 4
Eltz Castle

In the <u>West of Germany</u> between <u>Trier</u> and <u>Koblenz</u> lies Eltz Castle. Hidden in a small valley in the middle of a dense forest, the castle has been owned and occupied by the same family since the 12th century. The castle is extremely photogenic from afar, sitting on a rocky outcrop with a long bridge leading up to it. Many say <u>the castle is haunted</u> and past visitors have claimed to spot visions of medieval-era knights still guarding the grounds.

A guided tour allows visitors to gaze at the original furniture and art collection, with armour in the Knights' Hall dating back to the 16th century. Eltz Castle is relatively unknown and can be pleasantly uncrowded compared to other castles in Germany. The castle is only open for visitors between April and October.

What do the following words and phrases mean? Choose from the following list.

looking attractive on photographs,   a man who served the king or lord as a mounted soldier,   put in a place where it is unseen,   possessed and lived in,   a visitor's tour of a historic site,   closely packed,   ghosts in it,   from a great distance, in relation / comparison,   protecting / looking after,   a structure across a river,   stare at,   from the middle ages, rocks visible on the surface,   metal coverings to protect the body in battle,

1. hidden

2. dense

3. owned and occupied

4. photogenic

5. afar

6. outcrop

7. haunted

8. bridge

9. knight

10. medieval

11. guarding

12. guided tour

13. gaze

14. armour

15. relatively

Project 1: Find out as much as you can about a castle, palace, or fort in Germany. Write about 150 words.

Project 2: Write about 150 words on Eltz Castle.

THEME 7

TRADITIONS IN CUISINE AROUND THE WORLD

UNIT 1
Oman

Halwa is your classic everyday delicious Omani sweet made with fine semolina or cream of wheat (farina), sugar, ghee, nuts and flavored with cardamom powder. In Maharashtra, this sweet is called as Sheera. Semolina is called as suji, sooji or rava. This easy melt-in-the-mouth halwa recipe comes together in about 15 minutes. The recipe I share is a family heirloom recipe that we have been making for decades during family get-togethers, special occasions and festivals.

Heirloom *a piece of property that is inherited*

Project 1. Find out as much as you can about Halwa. Write about 100 words.

Project 2. Write about an Omani dish. Choose one that is not mentioned in the student's book or the workbook. Write about 150 words.

UNIT 2
Scotland

Originating in the northeastern part of Scotland in a small village named Cullen, this creamy smoked fish soup is another traditional Scottish dish. Cullen skink consists of smoked haddock, cream, potatoes, and onions, and is typically served with a side of toasted bread. While it originated as a local specialty of Cullen, you can find this popular soup on Scottish menus nationwide.

toasted bread *bread that has been browned by heat*

Project 1. Find out as much as you can about Cullen Skink. Write about 100 words.

Project 2. Write about a Scottish dish. Choose one that is not mentioned in the student's book or the workbook. Write about 150 words.

UNIT 3
France

Flamiche means 'cake' in Dutch and this dish originates from northern France, near the border with Belgium. It has a puff-pastry crust filled with cheese and vegetables and resembles a quiche. The traditional filling is leeks and cream, although various variations exist. There's also a pizza-like version of *flamiche,* which comes without the top crust of the pie. For a southern French twist, try the thin crusty *pissaladière,* which has anchovies, onions, and olives.

What do the following words and phrases mean? Choose from the following list.

small fish,   line dividing a country,   look alike,   a plant related to the onion family,   light flakey pastry,   a small quantity of something,   a baked tart

1. border

2. resemble

3. puff-pastry

4. quiche

5. leek

6. twist

7. anchovies

Project 1. Find out as much as you can about Flamiche. Write about 100 words.

Project 2. Write about a French dish. Choose one that is not mentioned in the student's book or the workbook. Write about 150 words.

UNIT 4
England

Spotted dick is a dense and delicious combination of sugar, flour, currants and the raw, shredded fat found around the loins and kidneys of a sheep. And if that's not sophisticated enough, it is traditionally drenched in the national beverage: custard.

What do these words and phrases mean? Choose from the following list.

the part of the body on both sides of the spine between the lowest ribs and the hip bones,   a dessert or sweet sauce made with milk and eggs,   cover thoroughly,   tear or cut into thin strips,   a drink,   having / revealing/ or involving a great deal of worldly experience and knowledge of things.

1. shred

2. loins

3. sophisticated

4. drench

5. beverage

6. custard

THEME 8

CLOTHES FROM AROUND THE WORLD

UNIT 1
Oman

The Omani turban is a kind of keffiyeh which Omanis wear wrapped around their head. This male accessory is the official cap in the country. The Omani turban names "massar" or "mazar" is very varied. It can be found in white cotton, thin embroidered wool or cashmere and also multicoloured. The turban permits to distinguish the peasant from a rich contractor. A distinction of tribes and classes that cannot be made as there are nearly 10 ways to wear the Omani turban.

What do these words and phrases mean? Choose from the following list.

many colours,   allow,   a kind of hat with a peak,   fine soft wool,   enclose in soft material,   having the approval or authorization of an authority or public body,   decorated with sewn on patterns,   someone who agrees to do a job or provide materials for a company

1. wrap

2. official

3. cap

4. embroidered

5. cashmere

FRANCIS A. ANDREW

6. muticoloured

7. permit

8. contractor

Project 1. Find out as much as you can about keffiyeh. Write about 100 words.

Project 2. Write about an item of Omani clothes. Choose one that is not mentioned in the student's book or the workbook. Write about 150 words.

UNIT 2
Wales

Traditional Welsh dress was worn by women in rural areas of Wales. The distinctive dress was based on a form of bedgown made from wool, of a style dating from the 18th century, worn over a corset. This was teamed with a printed neckerchief, a petticoat, apron and knitted stockings. The dress was completed by a high crowned hat reminiscent of 17th century fashions and a red, caped cloak.

What do the following words and phrases mean? Choose from the following list.

a tight fitting undergarment, brought together, a sleeveless cloak, a square of cloth worn round the neck, mark a fabric with a coloured design, a woman's short loose jacket formerly worn for general work., a protective garment worn over the front of one's clothes and tied at the back, the latest style of clothing, a covering for the legs, an outer skirt, reminding someone of something

1. bedgown

2. corset

3. printed

4. neckerchief

5. teamed

6. petticoat

7. apron

8. knitted stockings

9. reminiscent

10. fashion

11. cape

Project 1. Find out as much as you can about the Welsh gown. Write about 100 words.

Project 2. Write about an item of Welsh clothes. Choose one that is not mentioned in the student's book or the workbook. Write about 150 words.

UNIT 3
Spain

The **Gilet**: The word gilet comes from the Spanish word jileco (from Arabic word yalíka), or chaleco in modern Spanish. It is a sleeveless jacket, much like a waistcoat or vest that forms an important part of traditional Spanish clothing. Historically they were fitted and embroidered, and in the 19th century the gilet was a bodice shaped like a man's waistcoat. Contemporary gilets are used for additional warmth outdoors. In the first edition of *El Quixote*, in 1605, a diminutive of the word appeared: gilecuelo.

What do these words and phrases mean? Choose from the following list.

a garment for the upper body, the upper part of a woman's dress, the earliest appearance of a book, an undergarment worn on the upper part of the body, makes, a close fitting waist length garment, small

1. jacket

2. waistcoat

3. vest

4. forms

5. bodice

6. diminutive

7. fist edition

Project 1. Find out as much as you can about the Spanish gilet. Write about 100 words.

Project 2. Write about an item of Spanish clothes. Choose one that is not mentioned in the student's book or the workbook. Write about 150 words.

UNIT 4
Ireland

Nobles and freemen alike wore a leine.

The leine was a Celtic tunic that wide at the elbow on the sleeve and was wide at the bottom—often extending beyond the knees.

These were normally made of plain linen.

Both men and women wore leines, but those for women were longer.

The plain garment often had decorative embroidery around the neck, lower hem and sleeves in later years, or they might be sleeveless and plain.

What do these words and phrases mean? Choose from the following list.

the bottom of a garment, the joint between the upper arm and the forearm

1. elbow

2. hem

Project 1. Find out as much as you can about the Irish leine. Write about 100 words.

Project 2. Write about an item of Irish clothes. Choose one that is not mentioned in the student's book or the workbook. Write about 150 words.

THEME 9

TRADITIONAL MUSIC AND MUSICAL INSTRUMENTS AROUND THE WORLD

UNIT 1
Oman

The **music of <u>Oman</u>** has been strongly affected by the country's coastal location, with Omani sailors interacting with, and bringing back music from, <u>Egypt</u>, <u>Tanzania</u> and elsewhere. More recently, a <u>Portuguese</u> occupation has left its own marks, while geographic neighbours like the <u>United Arab Emirates</u>, <u>Yemen</u>, <u>Saudi Arabia</u> and <u>Iran</u> have also had a profound influence. In contrast to other Arab countries, Omani traditional music has a strong emphasis on <u>rhythm</u>.

Interact *communicate with*

Project: Find out as much as you can about Oman's traditional music. Write about 200 words.

UNIT 2
China

The erhu is a two-string, violin-like instrument that is played with a bow like a violin bow. It is also known as the Chinese violin in the Western world. Erhus are often played in Chinese opera performances and traditional orchestras.

bow *what is used to make music from a violin*

Project 1. Find out as much as you can about the Chinese erhu. Write about 100 words.

Project 2. Write about a Chinese musical instrument. Choose one that is not mentioned in the student's book or the workbook. Write about 150 words.

UNIT 3
Brazil

Agogô

The iron bells are typical of all Afro-Brazilian cultures. They give structure to the music and are struck with a stick. Depending on where the stick hits, different sounds are heard. The classical samba *agogô* consists of two bells, which are connected by an elastic round iron and can be pressed together. In this way, the characteristic click of the samba is heard. A special form are four-bell *agogôs* with four bells attached next to each other. They can be used to play more extensive melodies, such as those regularly heard in the sambodrome at the carnival in <u>Rio de Janeiro</u>.

What do these words and phrases mean? Choose from the following list.

something that can retain its normal shape after being stretched, a tune, a hollow metal object, typically in the shape of a deep inverted cup widening at the lip that sounds a clear musical note when struck, an exhibition place for the samba

1. bell

2. elastic

3. melody

4. sambodrome

Project 1. Find out as much as you can about the Agogo. Write about 100 words.

Project 2. Write about a Brazilian musical instrument. Choose one that is not mentioned in the student's book or the workbook. Write about 150 words.

UNIT 4
Sri Lanka

The hak gediya is one of Sri Lanka's most memorable musical instruments. It's usually made from a conch shell, which performers blow into in a slow and dramatic way to announce the start of ceremonial dances or events. As the dancer expels air into the shell, he theatrically widens his chest, throwing his head back before the long note ends.

What do these words and phrases mean? Choose from the following list.

a musical note that could be either twice or three times as long as a normal note, a tropical marine mollusc with a robust spiral shell, in an exaggerated and excessively dramatic manner, that will remain in the memory, a move creating an air current, give out information about something, send out

1. memorable

2. conch shall

3. blow

4. announce

5. expel

6. theatrically

7. long notes

Project 1. Find out as much as you can about the hak gediya. Write about 100 words.

Project 2. Write about a Sri Lankan musical instrument. Choose one that is not mentioned in the student's book or the workbook. Write about 150 words.

THEME 10

COMMUNICATION

UNIT 1
Satellite communication

A satellite is a communications system which can receive signals from Earth and retransmit those signals back. They retransmit the signals with a device called a transponder. A satellite can survive in space for 20 years.

The main components of a satellite consist of the communications system, which includes the antennas and transponders that receive and retransmit signals; the power system, which includes the solar panels that provide power - which they get from the sun. Satellites have propulsion systems. A satellite needs its own propulsion system to get to the right location above the Earth.

Some satellites are in geostationary orbit. That means, the satellite is located directly above the Earth's equator. It moves from west to east, synchronous with the rotation of the Earth.

Communication satellites range from microsatellites weighing less than 1 kg (2.2 pounds) to large satellites weighing over 6,500 kg (14,000 pounds). Advances in miniaturisation and digitalisation have substantially increased the capacity of satellites over the years. Early Bird had just one transponder capable of sending just one TV channel. The Boeing 702 satellites, can have more than 100 transponders. By using of digital compression technology, each transponder can have up to 16 channels, providing more than 1,600 TV channels through one satellite.

What do these words and phrases from the text mean? Choose from the following list.

the imaginary line that divides the Earth in half – into the northern hemisphere and the southern hemisphere,   a message, to send a signal / message by radio waves,   various individual things acting together to create a unified whole,   a part of a larger item,   to a large degree / to a great extent,   to continue in existence / not to die,   from one extreme to another / from the most to the least,   to be made up of / to be composed of, after the passage of many years,   to spin / to turn around and around,   to press or squeeze together,   to transmit back again, to drive or push something forward,   able to do something, to make something large very small / tiny,   a device made of metal for sending and receiving radio waves,   happening at the same time,   progress,   the maximum number or amount of something that can be stored somewhere,   changing / converting something to digital form

1.) transmit _____

2.) retransmit _____

3.) survive _____

4.) component _____

5.) consist _____

6.) antenna _____

7.) propulsion _____

8.) equator _____

9.) synchronous _____

10.) rotation _____

11.) range from – to _____

12.) advance _____

13.) miniaturisation _____

14.) digitalisation _____

15.) substantially _____

16.) capacity _____

17.) capable _____

18.) compression _____

19.) signal _____

20.) system _____

21.) over the years _____

Answer the questions in complete sentences.

1.) What is a satellite?

_____

_____

2.) How do satellites retransmit signals?

_____

_____

3.) How long can a satellite survive in space for?

_____

_____

4.) What are the main components of a satellite?

_____

_____

5.) Why does a satellite need a propulsion system?

_____

_____

6.) Where is a geostationary satellite located?

_____

_____

7.) In which direction does a geostationary satellite move?

_____

_____

8.) In what is it synchronous with?

_____

_____

9.) How much do microsatellites weight?

_____

_____

10.)What has greatly increased the capacity of satellites over the years?

_____

_____

Say if these sentences are true (T) or false (F)

1.) The antennas and transponders on a satellite receive and retransmit radio signals. _____

2.) The solar panels get their power from the Moon. _____

3.) The satellite finds its right location above the Earth by means of a propulsion system. _____

4.) Large satellites weigh over 14,000 kg. _____

5.) Early Bird had many transponders. _____

Choose *a*, *b*, *c* or *d*

1.) A satellite retransmits signals with a _____

   a.) solar panel   b.) transponder   c.) geostationary
   d.) propulsion

2.) Early Bird could send _____.

   a.) two TV channels   b.) 20 TV channels   c.) 1,600 TV channels   d.) one TV channel

3.) The Boeing 702 satellites can have more than _____transponders.

   a.) one hundred   b.) two hundred   c.) one thousand six hundred   d.) seven hundred and two

4.) A microsatellite can weigh less than _____ pounds.

   a.) 1.2 pounds   b.) 2.1 pounds   c.) 2.2 pounds   d.) 3.2 pounds

5.) Each transponder on a Boeing 702 satellite can have as many as _____ channels.

   a.) sixty   b.) sixteen   c.) sixty six   d.) sixty five

UNIT 2
How dolphins communicate.

Do dolphins talk to each other? It seems they do! Scientists all over the world have been studying dolphins for years, learning about the way they communicate with one another. In Hawaii, an experiment was performed between a mother dolphin and her young boy. Placed in two separate water tanks and connected via a special telephone, the two dolphins clearly communicated, chattering away with one another. This signifies that each dolphin has a recognisable "voice".

Dolphins are mammals and have many similarities to humans. Like humans, dolphins are social creatures, and are typically found in pods, swimming and hunting alongside other dolphins. They also appear to communicate with each other. Beginning when they are born, dolphins vocalise using squeaks, whistles, clicks, and other sounds. Researchers often observe dolphins chattering and being answered by another dolphin, indicating they are engaged in some sort of dialogue. At times, dolphins in the same pod make the same sounds in unison, further pointing to a communicative connection. In addition to vocalising, dolphins appear to communicate nonverbally through body language, blowing bubbles, and rubbing fins. Dolphins are playful creatures and like to splash people with water.

What do these words and phrases from the text mean? Choose from the following list.

a short, sharp sound, a type of marine animal, by way of, not using the voice, looking almost the same, participate, to make a sound like a voice, someone who does research / looks for information to be together in a community or group, put, containers for dolphins, to be a sign / to show, to point to, a part of a fish that sticks out from its side and uses for swimming, to look for something to kill and eat, to release air or gas suddenly, to do something to find out what the result it, talking incessantly, to look at, a high pitched shrill note, to take part in something, easy to know, how you see or perceive something,   to move along the surface of a body with pressure,   a species of animal of which its babies are nourished by the milk from their mothers,   a small globule usually hollow and light – often made with soap suds,   a living thing,   a conversation between two people,   done together as one body,   usual / normal,   to throw water at something or someone,   a short sharp shrill cry,   a container for storing water

1.) dolphin _____

2.) placed _____

3.) water tank _____

4.) via _____

5.) chattering _____

6.) signify _____

7.) recognisable _____

8.) mammal _____

9.) similarity _____

10.) social _____

11.) creature _____

12.) typical _____

13.) pods _____

14.) hunt _____

15.) appear _____

16.) vocalise _____

17.) indicate _____

18.) engage _____

19.) dialogue _____

20.) squeak _____

21.) whistle _____

22.) click _____

23.) observe _____

24.) researcher _____

25.) unison _____

26.) nonverbally _____

27.) blowing _____

28.) bubbles _____

29.) rub _____

30.) fin _____

31.) experiment _____

32.) engage _____

33.) splash _____

Answer these questions in complete sentences.

1.) Do Dolphins seem to talk to each other?

_____

_____

2.) Who have been studying dolphins for years?

_____

_____

3.) Where was an experiment performed?

_____

_____

4.) How were the two dolphins connected?

_____

_____

5.) What does each dolphin have?

_____

_____

6.) What are dolphins?

_____

_____

7.) How do dolphins vocalise?

_____

_____

8.) What do researchers often observe?

_____

_____

9.) How do dolphins communicate nonverbally?

_____

_____

10.) How are dolphins playful creatures?

_____

_____

Say if these sentences are true (T) or false (F)

1.) Scientists have been learning about the way dolphins communicate with each other._____

2.) An experiment was performed between a father dolphin and a mother dolphin. _____

3.) The two dolphins were in the same water tank. _____

4.) The two dolphins did not communicate with each other. _____

5.) Each dolphin has a recognisable voice. _____

Choose *a, b, c* or *d*

1.) Dolphins are mainly found _____.

a.) at the zoo   b.) at the circus   c.) in pods   d.) in a swimming pool

2.) They are _____ creatures.

a.) social   b.) human   c.) research   d.) voice

3.) Dolphins _____ in dialogue.

a.) pod   b.) engage   c.) swim   d.) experiment

4.) Dolphins have been observed _____.

   a.) chat   b.) chats   c.) chatter   d.) chattering

5.) Dolphins _____people with water.

   a.) splashes   b.) splash   c.) splashing   d.) to splash

UNIT 3
How birds communicate

The song of birds can be soothing and inspiring, but birds sing for more than just the beauty of it. Birds use song, call notes and behaviour to communicate with each other. Birds use sound and action to scare off predators or warn other birds about danger, to attract a mate or to defend one's territory.

Not all birds sing, but those that do are in a class of birds known as passerines, or perching birds. Many familiar birds are songbirds, including sparrows, wrens, warblers and thrushes. The males of the species often sing more than the females. The males sing to announce their presence and to let females know that they are available for mating. They also sing to defend the territory in which they mate, nest or feed. Females do not sing as frequently as the males. A song is often a multi-noted phrase that is repeated over and over. Some species only have one song in their repertoire, while other species may have several. Some birds, such as starlings, will mimic the songs of other species of birds, and they may be able to produce dozens of different songs.

Birds also communicate with their behavior. In many bird species, the male will dance, strut or put on some other performance to attract a female. Some birds, such as killdeer, fake an injury to lure predators away from their nests. Many other birds behave aggressively if their nest or territory is threatened and may attack the interlopers, even if they are much larger than the birds are.

UNIT 4
Native American smoke signals

Smoke Signals were used by many cultures including the Native American Indians as a means to quickly communicate visual messages over long distances. The simple messages sent via these signals were conveyed by means of columns or intermittent puffs or clouds of smoke.

Once a fire had been made smoke could be produced. The fire gave off smoke consisting of visible gases and fine particles given off by burning material. A wet blanket was used to cover the fire and when released produced a tower of black smoke that could be seen for miles.

The system used by Native American Indians for sending smoke signals was as follows:

- The first requirement was to select an area to set up a smoke signal system that was visible from a great distance
- Fuel was chosen for the fire that gave a dense, dark smoke

The Native Americans used smoke signals to communicate messages over long distances to a number of people.

The meanings of smoke signals varied. In general, there was not one set meaning as enemy tribes would also be able to read the messages that were being sent. if there were no enemies who could use the messages to their advantage then a simple code could be generally used. The simple code used for commonly understood smoke signals was:

- The meaning of one puff of smoke meant ATTENTION.
- The meaning of two puffs of smoke signalled ALL'S WELL
- The meaning of three puffs of smoke, or three fires in a row, signaled danger.

UNIT 5
How to communicate with a baby

Babies love to communicate with their own form of baby talk. And they hope you'll " baby talk" right back.

All through this first year, you can do a lot to encourage your baby's communication skills. And it's easy. All you need do is smile, talk, sing, and read to your baby.

Why focus on communicating with your baby? Because early speech and language skills are associated with success in developing reading, writing, and interpersonal skills, both later in childhood and later in life.

Baby Talk: Smile and Pay Attention

Long before they can speak clearly, babies understand the general meaning of what you're saying. They also absorb emotional tone. Encourage baby's early attempts to communicate with you with loving attention:

- Smile often at your baby, especially when they are cooing, gurgling, or otherwise vocalizing with baby talk.
- Look at your baby as they babble and laugh, rather than looking away, interrupting, or talking with someone else.
- Be patient as you try to decode your infant's baby talk and nonverbal communication, like facial expressions, gurgling, or babbling sounds that could signal either frustration or joy.
- Make time to give your baby lots of loving attention, so they can "speak" to you with their baby talk, even when you're busy with other tasks.

Baby Talk: Imitate Your Baby

Right from the start, baby talk should be a two-way street. By imitating your baby, you'll send an important message: what they are feeling and trying to communicate matters to you.

- Have back-and-forth conversations in baby talk to teach your baby the give-and-take of adult conversation.
- Imitate baby's vocalizations -- "ba-ba" or "goo-goo" -- then wait for them to make another sound and repeat that back.
- Do your best to respond, even when you don't understand what your baby is trying to say.
- Reinforce communication by smiling and mirroring facial expressions.
- Because gestures are a way babies try to communicate, imitate your baby's gestures, as well.

What do these words and phrases from the text mean? Choose from the following list.

to reflect back the same image, connected with, a sound which indicates the mood of a person, between persons, the time of your life when you are a child, to temporarily stop some action, clearing the throat with water, annoyed that something cannot be done, incoherent talk, / gibberish, take into so that it becomes part of something else, answer, happiness, communicating by moving the arms and hands, to focus on something without being distracted, to decipher what some cryptic message means, to do the same as someone else is doing, a way of saying that something can be effective on the giver as well as on the receiver, communicating by using movements of the body, being willing to wait, to make something stronger and more effective, communicating by movement of the face muscles, a piece of work,

1.) associated _____

2.) interpersonal _____

3.) childhood _____

4.) pay attention _____

5.) absorb _____

6.) emotional tone _____

7.) gurgling _____

8.) interrupt _____

9.) babble _____

10.) decode _____

11.) patient _____

12.) facial expressions _____

13.) frustration _____

14.) joy _____

15.) task _____

16.) body talk _____

17.) imitate _____

18.) respond _____

19.) two-way street _____

20.) mirroring _____

21.) reinforce _____

22.) gestures _____

Answer the questions in complete sentences.

1.) How do babies love to communicate?

_____

_____

2.) What do they hope?

_____

_____

3.) What do you do throughout the first year?

_____

_____

4.) What do you have to do?

_____

_____

5.) Why should you focus on communicating with your baby?

_____

_____

6.) What do babies understand before they can speak clearly?

_____

_____

7.) What do they absorb?

_____

_____

8.) When should you smile at your baby?

_____

_____

ENGLISH FOR UNIVERSITY ASPIRANTS

9.) When should you look at your baby?

_____

_____

10.) How should you be when you decode your infant's baby talk?

_____

_____

Say if these sentences are true (T) or false (F)

1.) You should not make time to give your baby loving attention.
_____

2.) Baby talk should only be for the baby but not for the adult.
_____

3.) "Ba ba" and "goo goo" are forms of baby vocalization. _____

4.) Respond to your baby even if you don't understand what the baby is saying. _____

5.) Never imitate facial expressions of your baby. _____

Choose *a, b, c* or *d*

1.) Gestures are a way babies _____.

a.) communicate   b.) communicates   c.) communication
d.) communications

2.) Babies want you to _____ to them.

a.) talks   b.) baby talk   c.) baby   d.) babies talk

3.) You can _____the baby's communication skills in the first year.

a.) encourages   b.) encouraging   c.) encourage
d.) to encourage

4.) Babies understand the general meaning of what you are saying _____they can speak.

a.) after   b.) when   c.) as   d.) before

5.) Always _____to your baby's baby talk.

a.) ignore   b.) laugh   c.) hear   d.) respond

READING FOR ENJOYMENT
Pigeon Post

While delivering messages on horseback or on foot was satisfactory, it also came with a lot of unpredictable variables, including dishonest messengers, accidents, loss of messages, unexpected delays, and a lack of guaranteed privacy. Therefore, not only was a faster delivery system desired, but also a more reliable one. Honestly, how fast can this tiny horse really run? What if the message is urgent?

More than 3,000 years ago, the first such improvement on message delivery was made, when homing pigeons were first introduced. While studying the patterns and movements of birds, it appeared that they had a wonderful sense of direction and could consistently find their way back to their nest. Even after foraging, hunting and soaring for miles in every direction, they were able to guide themselves home.

Pigeons tend to be easy to capture, quick to breed, relatively docile, and highly "in tune" with their sense of direction. In particular rock pigeons were chosen and interbred to create homing pigeons, essentially birds that could find their way "home". These pigeons would be trained very carefully, gradually being taken further and further from their "nests" before being released and flying home.

Answer these questions in complete sentences.

1.) What came with a lot of unpredictable variables?

_____

_____

2.) What kind of delivery system was required?

_____

_____

3.) How long ago was the first improvement on delivery made?

_____

_____

4.) What kind of pigeons were introduced?

_____

_____

5.) What kind of sense did these birds have?

_____

_____

6.) Where did they find their way back to?

_____

_____

7.) What do pigeons tend to be?

_____

_____

8.) What type of pigeons were interbred?

_____

_____

9.) How would these pigeons be trained?

_____

_____

10.)Where were they taken before being released?

_____

_____

THEME 11

TIME

UNIT 1
The Sundial

Sundial, the earliest type of timekeeping device, which indicates the time of day by the position of the shadow of some object from the sun's rays. As the day progresses, the sun moves across the sky, causing the shadow of the object to move and indicating the passage of time.

The first device for indicating the time of day was probably gnomon, dating from about 3500 BCE. It consisted of a vertical stick or pillar and the length of the shadow it cast gave an indication of the time of day. By the 8th century BCE more-precise devices were in use. The earliest known sundial still preserved is an Egyptian shadow clock dating from this period. The shadow clock consists of a straight base with a raised crosspiece at one end. The base, on which is inscribed a scale of six-time divisions, is placed in an east-west direction with the crosspiece at the east end in the morning and at the west end in the afternoon. The shadow of the crosspiece on this base indicates the time. Clocks of this kind were still in use in modern times in parts of Egypt.

Another early device was the hemispherical sundial, or hemicycle, attributed to the Greek astronomer Aristarchus about 280 BCE. Made of stone or wood, the instrument consisted of a cubical block into which an opening was cut. To this block a pointer was fixed with one end at the centre of the space. The path traveled by the tip of the pointer's shadow during the day was, approximately, a circular arc. The length and position of the arc varied according to the seasons, so an appropriate number of arcs was inscribed on the inside. Each arc was divided into 12 equal divisions, and each day was calculated from sunrise to sunset - it therefore had 12 equal intervals, or "hours." Because the length of the day varied according to the season, these hours varied in length from season to season and even from day to day and were called seasonal hours. Aristarchus's sundial was widely used for many centuries and, according to the Arab astronomer Al Battani, (*c.* 858–929 CE), was still in use in Muslim countries during the 10th century CE. The Babylonian astronomer, Berosus (*c.* 290 BCE) invented a variant of this sundial. Today, people often have sundials in their gardens, but they are merely ornamental.

What do these words and phrases from the text mean? Choose from the following list.

a division of the year – into four parts, only for decoration, a dark area caused by an object blocking the sun, a part of something, a break / period in between, Common Era, made high, a division of the sky between north and south, an object or machine that has been invented for a specific purpose, a way of measuring from lower to higher, used in many places, standing straight up, something that points in a direction, kept in existence, a curved movement, ly shaped like a circle, circa – about / approximately, to write something which is permanent on a material, something which is connected to a person or thing, only / just / no more than that, movement of time, something starting on a particular date, when the sun appears in the sky in the morning, when an object throws out a shadow when it blocks the sun, to point to something and identify it, when the sun is disappearing from the sky in the evening, the bottom of something, Before the Common Era, a horizontal part of something, a very narrow route for one person to walk on, to differ, a beam of light from the sun, the point of something, a long vertical column to support a horizontal crossbar, a scientist who studies objects in the Universe, a long thin piece of wood, the movement of the time of the day, what something contains, a solid of six equal square sides

1.) device _____

2.) c _____

3.) CE _____

4.) BCE _____

5.) indicate _____

6.) shadow _____

7.) ray _____

8.) the day progresses _____

9.) passage of time _____

10.) vertical _____

11.) stick _____

12.) pillar _____

13.) cast a shadow _____

14.) raised _____

15.) crosspiece _____

16.) preserved _____

17.) consist _____

18.) dating from _____

19.) base _____

20.) inscribe _____

21.) scale _____

22.)division _____

23.)hemisphere _____

24.)attribute _____

25.)astronomer _____

26.)cube _____

27.)pointer _____

28.)path _____

29.)tip _____

30.)arc _____

31.)circular _____

32.)vary _____

33.)season _____

34.)sunrise _____

35.)sunset _____

36.)interval _____

37.)widely used _____

38.)merely _____

39.)ornamental _____

Answer the questions in complete sentences.

1.) What is the earliest type of time-keeping device?

_____

_____

2.) How does a sundial indicate the time?

_____

_____

3.) When was the gnomon used?

_____

_____

4.) What did the length of the shadow of the gnomon indicate?

_____

_____

5.) When were more precise devices used?

_____

_____

6.) What is the earliest known sundial that is still preserved?

_____

_____

7.) What is the name of the device that is attributed to Aristarchus?

_____

_____

8.) What was it made of?

_____

_____

9.) What was each arc divided into?

_____

_____

10.) Who invented a variant of this sundial?

_____

_____

Say if these sentences are true (T) or false (F)

1.) As the day progresses, the sun stands still in the sky. _____

2.) The first device consisted of a horizontal stick or pillar. _____

3.) The Egyptian Shadow clock dates from 8th century BCE. _____

4.) The hemispherical sundial is a different device than the hemicycle. _____

5.) The length of a day changes with the seasons. _____

Choose *a, b, c* or *d*

1.) During the day, the sun moves across the _____.

a.) Moon   b.) stars   c.) sundial   d.) sky

2.) The block in the hemispherical sundial was _____

    a.) a cube   b.) a circle   c.) a rectangle   d.) a triangle

3.) Al Battani was an _____ astronomer.

    a.) Babylonian   b.) Arab   c.) Greek   d.) Roman

4.) The Babylonian astronomer mentioned in the text is called _____.

    a.) Aristarchus   b.) Al Battani   c.) Berosus   d.) Newton

5.) In the modern world, sundials are _____.

    a.) for telling the time   b.) for finding the position of the sun   c.) to find the length of the day   d.) for ornaments

UNIT 2
Water Clocks

For a more exact measurement of time, the ancient Egyptians developed a water clock made from stone, copper, or pottery. The Greeks referred to it as a *klepsydra* which means a "water thief". An inscription on the tomb of Amenemhet, a court official who lived c.1500 BC, stated that he was the inventor of the water clock. The earliest examples date to around the same time, c1550–1295 BC.

The *klepsydra* is essentially a wide vessel with a hole at the bottom that could be plugged. In order to keep time at night, the vessel was filled with water, which was then allowed to drain. The water would take exactly twelve hours to pour through the hole; marks on the inside of the vessel's walls marked the precise hours as the water level decreased. This way, Egyptian mathematicians were assured that they could perform the necessary duties at the correct hour.

Water clocks became a common method of telling time in the ancient world. The "Tower of Winds" in Athens, built in the early first century BC, is a marvel of engineering, containing both sundials and a water clock inside. This monument can still be seen in Athens today.

Water clocks were also used to time events. From at least the fourth century BC, water clocks were used in court houses to make sure that speakers stayed within their allotted time to talk. This practice was also adopted by the more litigious Romans in their own courts and ensured that proceedings moved along at a steady pace.

Hellenistic astronomers of the last few centuries BC, who still used the Egyptian system of dividing the day into 24 hours, began dividing the hours into sixty minutes for more accurate time-keeping, following the Babylonian system of counting. This system survived the middle ages and is still used today.

What do these words and phrases from the text mean? Choose from the following list.

someone who works for the court – a kind of lawyer, to function / to do something, relating to the Greeks, the art of making things with clay – mixing water and sand, usual / normal / regular / ordinary, a small area on a surface having a different colour from its surroundings, very old, the building where legal cases are heard and judged, a special piece of writing on a book / a monument / a piece of wood etc, a one hundred year period, a way of doing something, to be exact, to mention or point to something, working with machines or mechanical devices, most importantly, a system / order of doing things, something wonderful / amazing, a place where a dead person is buried, an obligation / something you must do, a kind of metal, not changing from fast to slow but going at the same speed, a round opening in the ground or in a container, to m=be made to feel confident about something, someone who makes something never made before – he / she is the first person to make it, a structure commemorating a person or an event, the movement of water out of a place or container, to take something for yourself – a child / an idea / a system etc, get smaller / less, a given amount of time – no more,   *someone who studies / teaches mathematics,*   *a container – usually for liquid,*   *something to cover a hole to stop the liquid draining away,*   *a person always resorting to the law*

1.) ancient _____

2.) copper _____

3.) pottery _____

4.) refer _____

5.) inscription _____

6.) tomb _____

7.) court official _____

8.) inventor _____

9.) essentially _____

10.) vessel _____

11.) hole _____

12.) plug _____

13.) drain _____

14.) mark _____

15.) precise _____

16.) decrease _____

17.) mathematician _____

18.) assured _____

19.) perform _____

20.)duty _____

21.) common _____

22.)method _____

23.)marvel _____

24.)monument _____

25.)engineering _____

26.)court house _____

27.)allotted time _____

28.)adopt _____

29.)litigious _____

30.)proceedings _____

31.) steady pace _____

32.)Hellenistic _____

33.)century _____

Answer the questions in complete sentences.

1.) Why did the ancient Egyptians develop a water clock?

_____

_____

2.) Which materials did they use for making this clock?

_____

_____

3.) Who was Amenemhet?

_____

_____

4.) How long did the water take to pour through the hole in the vessel?

_____

_____

5.) What did the water clock become in the ancient world?

_____

_____

6.) Where was 'The Tower of Winds?'

_____

_____

7.) How were water clocks used in court houses?

_____

_____

8.) How many hours did the ancient Egyptians divide the day into?

_____

_____

9.) How many minutes did the ancient Egyptians divide the hours into?

_____

_____

10.)Is this system still in use today?

_____

_____

Say if these sentences are true (T) or false (F)

1.) Water clocks give a more exact measurement of time. _____

2.) The Greeks called the water clock a 'water thief.' _____

3.) The hole at the bottom of the water clock can't be plugged. ____

4.) The exact hours could not be calculated. _____

5.) The "Tower of Winds' can no longer be seen in Greece today. _____

Choose *a, b, c* or *d*

1.) The water clock could be made up of _____metal (s).

a.) two   b.) three   c.) one   d.) four

2.) The water took _____hours to drain through the hole.

a.) 12   b.) 6   c.) 13   d.) 9

3.) The "Tower of Winds' was built in the _____.

a.) first century AD   b.) the second century BC   c.) the third century AD   d.) the first century BC

4.) Water clocks were used to time _____.

a.) courts   b.) litigious Romans   c.) events   d.) Romans

5.) The system survived _____.

    a.) the Dark Ages   b.) the Middle Ages   c.) many ages   d.) ages

UNIT 3
The Mechanical Clock

Mechanical clocks replaced the old water clocks, which, by the 13th century, had been around for millennia.

What makes a mechanical clock is a mechanism called an escapement -- the balance wheel on a watch or the pendulum on a grandfather clock. An escapement ticks in a steady rhythm and lets the gears move forward in a series of little equal jumps.

The first escapement was the *verge and foliot* mechanism (see the full image opposite). The foliot is a horizontal bar with weights on either end. It sits on a vertical rod, called a verge. The verge has pallets to release the main gear which is turned by a heavy stone on the end of a cable.

It was complex and very creative, but when was it invented? We don't really know. People who wrote about early clocks couldn't see that the escapement was more than just an incremental improvement on the water clock. It was a whole new technology.

French architect Villard de Honnecourt described the first escapement in AD 1250; but he didn't yet use it to control a clock. Instead, he built a kind of *almost-clock* -- a gadget that followed the sun as it moved across the sky.

The first clear drawing of an escapement was given by Jacopo di Dondi and his son in 1364. They'd probably been building clocks for twenty years before that. So we can only guess that the first mechanical clocks were made in the late 13th century.

What do these words and phrases from the text mean? Choose from the following list.

a conjecture / to say something without any information, a level surface in a clock or watch, an upgrade / made better, to put something in place of another thing, a person who designs buildings, something produced or operated by a machine, complicated / not easy or straight-forward, a body suspended from a fixed point so as to swing freely to and fro, more advanced than a sundial or a water clock but still not a mechanical clock, to let something go free, in multiples of a thousand years, a mechanical or electronic device, a regular and recurring movement, moveable part of a machine, the noise a clock makes rhythmically, a wire or rope of great strength, in small stages

1.) mechanical _____

2.) replace _____

3.) millennia _____

4.) pendulum _____

5.) tick _____

6.) rhythm _____

7.) gear _____

8.) complex _____

9.) pallet _____

10.) release _____

11.) cable _____

12.) incremental _____

13.) architect _____

14.) improvement _____

15.) almost – clock _____

16.) gadget _____

17.) guess _____

Answer the questions in complete sentences.

1.) Which clocks did mechanical clocks replace?

_____

_____

2.) What makes a mechanical clock?

_____

_____

3.) How does an escapement tick?

_____

_____

4.) Where does the foliot sit?

_____

_____

5.) Who first described the escapement?

_____

_____

6.) In what year did he describe it?

_____

_____

7.) What kind of clock did he build?

_____

_____

8.) Who gave the first clear drawing of an escapement?

_____

_____

9.) In which year was it drawn?

_____

_____

10.) How many years had they been building before they made the drawing?

_____

_____

Say if these sentences are true (T) or false (F)

1.) By the 13th century, mechanical clocks had been around for millennia. _____

2.) A watch has a pendulum. _____

3.) An escarpment lets the gears to backwards in little jumps. _____

4.) A foliot has weights on either end. _____

5.) Mechanical clocks were a new technology. _____

Choose *a*, *b*, *c* or *d*

1.) Water clocks were replaced by _____.

   a.) mechanical clocks   b.) pendulums   c.) foliots
   d.) weights

2.) Balance wheels and pendulums are _____.

   a.) clocks   b.) water clocks   c.) weights   d.) escapements

3.) The foliot is a _____ bar.

   a.) vertical   b.) horizontal   c.) pendulum   d.) balance wheel

4.) People thought the escapement was _____improvement.

   a.) a major   b.) a great   c.) a small   d.) no

5.) We _____that the first mechanical clocks were made in the 13th century.

   a.) know for sure   b.) definitely know   c.) certainly know
   d.) can only conjecture

UNIT 4
Watches

Watches have been with us for a long, long time. But what exactly is the history of watches? Watches today are not what they used to be. Take a look at a smartphone for example. What we know is that it can take calls, send texts, and carry out scores of other functions. With all this highly advanced technology, it is interesting to look back throughout history and understand where watches came from.

Today, watches are worn on the wrist. But when watches were first invented in the 16th century, they were not worn on the wrist, they were kept in the pocket. Like the first clocks, they only had the hour hand. In the 17th century minute and second hands were added.

Although wrist watches have existed for centuries, it was only wealthy people who could afford them. During the First World War, army officers did not want to keep taking a watch out of their pockets when they needed to know the time. It was more convenient for them to look at the time from a watch on their wrists. After the war in 1918, wearing wrist watches by civilians became more and more popular.

In the last twenty years, computers have been getting smaller and smaller. First, they went from the size of entire rooms to personal computers. Next, we developed laptops and smartphones. Now, in the modern age, we can fit advanced computers in tiny compartments that fit on our wrists. The result is smartwatches like the Apple Watch. There is still a large market for vintage style watches, but smart innovations are changing the watch industry in a rapid way.

When you go shopping for watches online, most of the pieces you come across are vastly different than timepieces were throughout history. The reason is that what you see of watches today is the accumulation of hundreds of years of advancements. Now, whoever you are and whatever you are looking for, there is a piece for you. You just have to go find it.

What do these words and phrases from the text mean? Choose from the following list.

any device which shows the time, a moving bar on a clock or watch which marks off the seconds, what something does, a gradual gathering together of many things over a period of time, 20, a superior soldier, comfortable and fitting in well with a person's situation, very modern and well developed, a section, a moving bar on a watch or clock marking off the minutes, extremely small, a part of the body between the hand and the arm, liked by a great many people, a moving bar on a clock or a watch marking off the hours, covering a

*very wide area,   having being / having reality,   complete /
total,   old-fashioned / not modern,   not having enough money
to buy something,   someone who is not a soldier / not in the
army,   like an invention*

1.) score _____

2.) function _____

3.) highly advanced _____

4.) wrist _____

5.) the hour hand _____

6.) the minute hand _____

7.) the second hand _____

8.) exist _____

9.) can afford _____

10.) army officer _____

11.) convenient _____

12.) civilian _____

13.) popular _____

14.) entire _____

15.) compartment _____

16.) vintage _____

17.) innovation _____

18.) tiny _____

19.) vast _____

20.)timepiece _____

21.)accumulation _____

Answer the questions in complete sentences

1.) How long have watches been with us?

_____

_____

2.) What can smartphones do?

_____

_____

3.) Where are watches worn today?

_____

_____

4.) When were watches first invented?

_____

_____

5.) Where did people keep their watches?

_____

_____

6.) What hand did the first watches have?

_____

_____

7.) Who could afford the first wrist watches?

_____

_____

8.) Why did army officers during the First World War wear wrist watches?

_____

_____

9.) In which year did the First World War end?

_____

_____

10.) What has been happening to computers over the last twenty years?

_____

_____

Say if these sentences are true (T) or false (F)

1.) Minute and second hands were added to watches in the seventeenth century. _____

2.) Wrist watches have exited for only one hundred years. _____

3.) In World War 1, army officers did not like looking at wrist watches. _____

4.) Early computers needed entire rooms. _____

5.) Nowadays there is no market for vintage style watches. _____

Choose *a, b, c* or *d*

1.) Watches nowadays are _____ what they used to be?

a.) the same as   b.) different to   c.) on the wrist   d.) in the pocket

2.) After personal computers came _____.

a.) laptops and watches   b.) smartphones and computers taking up entire rooms   c.) laptops and wrist watches   d.) laptops and smartphones

3.) Apple Watch is _____

a.) a smartwatch   b.) a vintage watch   c.) a 17th century watch   d.) an hour hand watch

4.) Smart innovations are changing the watch industry in _____ way,

a.) a slow   b.) an easy   c.) fast   c.) vintage

5.) The modern watch is an accumulation of _____ advancements.

a.) a century of   b.) a hundred years of   c.) years of
d.) hundreds of years of

UNIT 5
Big Ben

The **Houses of Parliament** and Elizabeth Tower, commonly called Big Ben, are among London's most famous landmarks and must-see **London attractions**. Technically, Big Ben is the name given to the massive **bell** inside the clock tower, which weighs more than 13 tons (13,760 kg). The clock tower looks spectacular at night when the four clock faces are illuminated. It is probably the most famous clock in the world.

The Palace of Westminster was destroyed by fire in 1834. In 1844, it was decided the new buildings for the Houses of Parliament should include a tower and a clock. A massive bell was required. Big Ben first rang across Westminster (a part of London) on 31 May 1859. A short time later, in September 1859, Big Ben cracked. A lighter hammer was fitted and the bell rotated to present an undamaged section to the hammer. This is the bell as we hear it today.

Elizabeth Tower stands at more than 96 metres (105yrds) tall, with 334 steps to climb up to the belfry and 399 steps to the Ayrton Light at the very top of the tower.

Big Ben is found in the Elizabeth Tower at the north end of The Houses of Parliament in Westminster, Central London, next to the River Thames.

In August 2017, refurbishment work commenced on Elizabeth Tower and Big Ben. The work lasted for three years. During this time, the tower was scaffolded, and the clock mechanism was stopped for several months (no chiming or striking). The refurbishment is now complete, and the Elizabeth Tower is now open to visitors.

What do these words and phrases from the text mean? Choose from the following list.

renovate / redecorate,   don't miss it / it is important to see it, to move in a circular motion,   huge / very big / enormous,   lit up / made bright with lights,   part of a bell tower (steeple) in which a bell is kept,   the sound of a bell,   exactly / precisely, a temporary structure outside a building used when workers are doing repairs to the building,   one unit of a stair where a foot is placed when climbing,   one unit of sound from a bell,   something which interests people / it brings people to see it,   amazing / wonderful / fantastic,   a hollow object that gives a clear musical ring when struck,   a long thin zig-zag damage on something,   begin / start,   a very tall and narrow building, need

1.) must-see _____

2.) attraction _____

3.) technically _____

4.) bell _____

5.) tower _____

6.) massive _____

7.) spectacular _____

8.) illuminated _____

9.) require _____

10.) crack _____

11.) ring / rang _____

12.) rotate _____

13.) step _____

14.) belfry _____

15.) refurbish _____

16.) commence _____

17.) scaffolding _____

18.) chime _____

Answer the questions in complete sentences

1.) What are the Houses of Parliament and Elizabeth Tower commonly called?

_____

_____

2.) What exactly is Big Ben?

_____

_____

3.) How much does Big Ben weigh?

_____

_____

4.) How many clock faces are there?

_____

_____

5.) What happened in 1834?

_____

_____

6.) What happened ten years later?

_____

_____

7.) When did Big Ben first ring across Westminster?

_____

_____

8.) When did Big Ben crack?

_____

_____

9.) How tall is Elizabeth Tower?

_____

_____

10.) How many steps are there up to the belfry?

_____

_____

Say if these sentences are true (T) or false (F)

1.) There are 334 steps to the Ayrton Light. _____

2.) Big Ben is located in the Ayrton Light. _____

3.) London is a part of Westminster. _____

4.) In September 2017, refurbishment work started on Elizabeth Tower and Big Ben. _____

5.) The clock mechanism was stopped. _____

Choose *a*, *b*, *c* or *d*

1.) During refurbishment, the Tower was _____.

   a.) scaffold   b.) scaffolding   c.) scaffolds   d.) scaffolded

2.) The refurbishment work took _____ years.

   a.) three   b.) two   c.) four   d.) five

3.) Now, the refurbishment is _____

    a.) unfinished   b.) incomplete   c.) finished   d.) ongoing

4.) The Elizabeth Tower is _____to visitors.

    a.) closed   b.) open   c.) stopped   d.) finished

5.) Elizabeth Tower is at the _____end of the Houses of Parliament.

    a.) south   b.) east   c.) west d) north

READING FOR ENJOYMENT
Clouds

All clouds are made up of basically the same thing: <u>water droplets or ice crystals</u> that float in the sky. But all clouds look a little bit different from one another, and sometimes these differences can help us predict a change in the weather.

Here's a list of some of the most common cloud types you might spot in the sky:

High Clouds (16,500-45,000 feet)

Cirrus

Cirrus clouds are delicate, feathery clouds that are made mostly of ice crystals. Their wispy shape comes from wind currents which twist and spread the ice crystals into strands.

Weather prediction: A change is on its way!

Cirrostratus

Cirrostratus clouds are thin, white clouds that cover the whole sky like a veil. These clouds are most commonly seen in the

winter, and can cause the appearance of a halo around the sun or the moon.

Weather prediction: Rain or snow will arrive within 24 hours!

Cirrocumulus

Cirrocumulus clouds are thin, sometimes patchy, sheet-like clouds. They sometimes look like they're full of ripples or are made of small grains.

Weather prediction: Fair, but cold. However, if you live in a tropical region, these clouds could be a sign of an approaching hurricane!

Mid-level Clouds (6,500-23,000 feet)

Altocumulus

Altocumulus clouds have several patchy white or gray layers, and seem to be made up of many small rows of fluffy ripples. They are lower than cirrus clouds, but still quite high. They are made of liquid water, but they don't often produce rain.

Weather prediction: Fair

Altostratus

Altostratus clouds are gray or blue-gray mid-level clouds composed of ice crystals and water droplets. The clouds usually cover the entire sky.

Weather prediction: Be prepared for continuous rain or snow!

Nimbostratus

Nimbostratus clouds are dark, gray clouds that seem to fade into falling rain or snow. They are so thick that they often blot out the sunlight.

Weather prediction: Gloomy with continuous rain or snow

Low Clouds (less than 6,500 feet)

Cumulus

Cumulus clouds look like fluffy, white cotton balls in the sky. They are beautiful in sunsets, and their varying sizes and shapes can make them fun to observe!

Weather prediction: Fair

Stratus

Stratus cloud often look like thin, white sheets covering the whole sky. Since they are so thin, they seldom produce much rain or snow. Sometimes, in the mountains or hills, these clouds appear to be fog.

Weather prediction: Fair, but gloomy

Cumulonimbus

Cumulonimbus clouds grow on hot days when warm, wet air rises very high into the sky. From far away, they look like huge mountains or towers.

Weather prediction: Look out for rain, hail, and tornadoes!

Stratocumulus

Stratocumulus clouds are patchy gray or white clouds that often have a dark honeycomb-like appearance.

Weather prediction: Fair weather for now, but a storm might be on its way.

Special Clouds

Contrails

Contrails are made by high-flying jet airplanes. They are still clouds, though, because they are made of water droplets condensed from the water vapor in the exhaust of the jet engines.

Weather prediction: Contrails can provide information about the layers of moisture in the sky.

Mammatus clouds

Mammatus clouds are actually altocumulus, cirrus, cumulonimbus, or other types of clouds that have these pouch-like shapes hanging out of the bottom. The pouches are created when cold air within the cloud sinks down toward the Earth.

Weather prediction: Severe weather might be on its way!

Orographic clouds

Orographic clouds get their shape from mountains or hills that force the air to move over or around them. They can also be formed by sea breezes and often appear as lines where two air masses meet.

Weather prediction: An early sign that the conditions might be right to form afternoon thunderstorms!

Lenticular clouds

Lenticular clouds are shaped like lenses or almonds or...flying saucers! They may get their shape from hilly terrain or just the way the air is rising over flat terrain.

Weather prediction: None!

The <u>GOES-16</u> (Geostationary Operational Environmental Satellite-16) satellite can watch clouds with a new instrument called the Advanced Baseline Imager, or ABI for short. Scientists have found that rapid growth and cooling at the tops of clouds are indicators of the potential for severe weather. The ABI can show more detailed changes in cloud-top features, helping scientists assess the potential size and severity of a storm even before it reaches its peak!

Answer the questions in complete sentences

1.) What are clouds made of?

_____

_____

2.) How high are cirrus clouds?

_____

_____

3.) How do cirrus clouds obtain their wispy shapes?

_____

_____

4.) Which clouds get their shape from mountains and hills?

_____

_____

5.) Which clouds look like fluffy cotton balls in the sky?

_____

_____

6.) Which clouds have no weather predictions?

_____

_____

7.) Which clouds indicate that severe weather is on its way?

_____

_____

8.) Which clouds are patchy, grey or white?

_____

_____

9.) What is the name of the instrument which can watch clouds?

_____

_____

10.) What is GOES?

_____

_____

FARMING

UNIT 1
The Poultry Farm

A poultry farm is where domesticated birds are raised. Poultry include chickens, turkey, ducks, and geese. These animals are raised for their meat and eggs. Chickens are the most common bird raised for both meat and eggs. Chickens that are raised for their meat are called broilers. Chickens that are raised for their eggs are called laying hens or layers. Some special breeds of poultry are raised for shows and competitions.

Following are poultry farm activities:

It is very important to prepare the chicken house for the arrival of the chicks. Then it is essential to feed the chicks. It is necessary to monitor the conditions inside the chicken houses. The temperature, humidity and air quality must be regularly checked. It is vital to monitor the health of the chickens. Cleaning the coops is a way of ensuring a hygienic environment for the chickens. Another thing that must be done is to collect the eggs of the laying hens. Meat chickens must be loaded on to trucks for transportation to chicken plants.

Commercial duck farms are operations similar to chicken farms. Duck meat production is therefore a full-time business requiring investment in both time and money. While duck farming is quite small in comparison to chicken farming, it is expanding rapidly, with increasing global demand. This makes duck farming an attractive option for those considering it as a career. There are more than 40 breeds of domestic ducks, but the Pekin duck is the most common variety raised for eggs and meat.

Geese are mainly kept for meat production, so the breeding birds are selected based on their quick growth, early-maturity and meaty bodies. There are differences in breeds of geese, so their characteristics should be evaluated in order to best meet the producer's requirements. If birds are to be kept for breeding, then egg production and reproductive efficiency are important things to look at. If the geese are raised only for market, the market's meat production and body requirements are of major importance.

An average turkey farm produces six to seven thousand turkeys, three times a year. A hatching egg farm will raise the breeding turkeys to produce eggs that are collected, sanitized and shipped to a turkey hatchery. The hatchery will then hatch the eggs into young turkeys (or poults), which will then be shipped to commercial turkey farms, where they are housed and raised into adult turkeys. Once the turkeys reach a desired market weight, they are transported to the processor. This growing cycle usually runs until the turkeys grow to be 10-18 weeks of age.

What do these words and phrases from the text mean? Choose from the following list.

a newly born chicken,   features,   not wild animals / animals which have been trained,   to see how things are similar to each other and how they differ,   to make something clean,   to put things on to a truck for transportation,   to think about, types of animals,   chosen,   to bring animals up from birth to adulthood,   when a chicken comes out of its egg,   to follow the movement and progress of something,   money put into a business,   regular / normal / nothing special,   at full growth, a building where chickens are kept,   demand from all over the world / international demand,   clean and healthy,   to produce like itself

1.) domesticated animals _____

2.) raise animals _____

3.) breeds of animals _____

4.) chick _____

5.) monitor _____

6.) coop _____

7.) hygienic _____

8.) load on to a truck _____

9.) global demand _____

10.) investment _____

11.) comparison _____

12.) consider _____

13.) selected _____

14.) maturity _____

15.) characteristics_____

16.) reproduce _____

17.) hatch _____

18.) hatchery _____

19.) sanitize _____

20.) average _____

Answer the questions in complete sentences

1.) What is raised on a poultry farm?

_____

_____

2.) What is a broiler?

_____

_____

3.) What are layers?

_____

_____

4.) Which three things should be regularly checked inside a chicken house?

_____

_____

5.) What must be collected from the laying hens?

_____

_____

6.) What does duck meat production require?

_____

_____

7.) How many breeds of domestic ducks are there?

_____

_____

8.) How many turkeys does an average turkey farm produce?

_____

_____

9.) What will a turkey hatchery do?

_____

_____

10.) How long does the growing cycle last?

_____

_____

Say if these sentences are true (T) or false (F)

1.) Cows and sheep are poultry. _____

2.) Chickens are the most common bird raised for meat and eggs. _____

3.) Ordinary breeds of poultry and raised for shows and competitions. _____

4.) Duck meat production is a part-time business. _____

5.) Geese are mainly kept for their eggs. _____

Choose *a, b, c* or *d*

1.) It is essential to _____the conditions inside the chicken houses.

a.) monitor   b.) monitors   c.) monitoring   d.) monitorings

2.) Meat chickens are loaded on to _____.

    a.) coops   b.) trucks   c.) trains   d.) chicken houses

3.) Duck farming is _____expanding.

    a.) rapid   b.) rapids   c.) rapidly   d.) rapidity

4.) A hatchery _____the turkey eggs.

    a.) hatch   b.) hatching   c.) hatchings   d.) hatches

5.) The growing cycle runs until the turkeys are _____ weeks.

    a.) 8 – 10   b.) 10 – 80   c.) 10 – 18   d.) 8 – 18

UNIT 2
An Urban Farm

Urban growth could become problematic in terms of feeding the population. In response to the need for food and the growing demand for local food to reduce the impact on the environment, current farming practices needed to be redesigned. Urban and peri-urban farming was the result. It consists of producing vegetables, fruit and other food or raising animals in and around cities.

According to the Food and Agriculture Organisation (FAO), which advocates urban farming, more than 800 million people are engaged in urban and peri-urban agriculture worldwide. It may take the form of shared vegetable gardens on rooftops or in public spaces. It has numerous advantages: it helps feed people in the city, produces fresh local produce, helps green cities by sequestering carbon and limiting urban heat islands, creates social ties, creates jobs, enhances the value of empty spaces, enriches the city's biodiversity, and more.

Based on a circular economy approach and its traditional business lines, a company called Veolia is actively involved in various urban farming projects through its Fertile Cities projects:

- **Permaculture:** a form of cultivation aimed at producing a large quantity of fruit and vegetables on a small plot of land by imitating the way nature works (without pesticides, synthetic fertilizers or mechanically working the soil, etc.).
- **Bio-intensive micro-market gardening in permaculture:** cultivation of organic vegetables on a small plot of land imitating the way nature works.
- **Aquaponics:** a form of cultivation combining fish and plants to recreate an ecosystem in an aquarium.
- **Aquaculture:** a form of aquatic agriculture that allows species such as fish to be raised.

What do these words and phrases from the text mean? Choose from the following list.

farming done in or close to an urban community, relating to a city or town, join together, make bigger and better, a large tank for fish, to design something again and different to what it was before, to copy someone or something else / to mimic, to separate / isolate / hide away, something or someone who gives problems, effect, biologically productive, to argue in favour of / to speak favourably of something, to add more to something to make it better, made from artificial substances – not by nature, a chemical element with the symbol C, chemical or natural substances added to soil to make plants grow faster, a variety of plants and animals, many / a lot of, related to water, using natural rather than chemicals to enhance plant growth, to be connected to some activity / to be part of an activity, growing things in the soil, a place where plants and animals support each other in an interconnected cycle of life, a section of land, a chemical used to kills insects which attack crops

1.) urban _____

2.) problematic _____

3.) impact _____

4.) redesign _____

5.) peri-urban farming _____

6.) advocate _____

7.) engaged in _____

8.) numerous _____

9.) sequester _____

10.) carbon _____

11.) cultivation _____

12.) fertile _____

13.) enhance _____

14.) biodiversity _____

15.) enrich _____

16.) plot of land _____

17.) fertilizer _____

18.) imitate _____

19.) pesticide _____

20.) synthetic _____

21.) ecosystem _____

22.) aquarium _____

23.) aquatic _____

24.) combine _____

25.) organic _____

Answer the questions in complete sentences

1.) How could urban growth become problematic?

_____

_____

2.) Why did current farming practices need to be redesigned?

_____

_____

3.) What was the result of the redesign?

_____

_____

4.) What do urban and peri-urban farming consist of?

_____

_____

5.) How many people are engaged in urban and peri-urban farming worldwide?

_____

_____

6.) Where might you find this type of farming?

_____

_____

7.) What are the advantages of this type of farming?

_____

_____

8.) On what does Veolia base its farming projects?

_____

_____

9.) What is the name of Veolia's projects?

_____

_____

10.) What things does permaculture never use?

_____

_____

Say if these sentences are true (T) or false (F)

1.) Permaculture aims at producing large quantities of fruit and vegetables. _____

2.) Permaculture does not imitate the way nature works. _____

3.) Bio-intensive micro-market gardening imitates the way nature works. _____

4.) Aquaponics is performed on a farm. _____

5.) Aquaponics uses fish and plants. _____

Choose *a, b, c* or *d*

1.) The FAO is _____

a.) The Fish and Agriculture Organisation
b.) The Food and Aquatic Organisation
c.) The Food and Agriculture Organisation
d.) The Fish and Aquatic Organisation

2.) Permaculture requires a _____plot of land.

a.) small   b.) large   c.) medium sized   d.) huge

3.) In bio-intensive micro-market gardening, _____ vegetables are grown.

a.) chemical   b.) micro   c.) garden   d.) organic

4.) Aquaponics is _____in an aquarium.

a.) a garden   b.) an ecosystem   c.) organic   d.) aquatic

5.) Species of fish are raised in _____.

a.) peri-urban farming   b.) organic agriculture
c.) aquaculture   d.) aquatic

UNIT 3
Rice Farm

Before rice can be planted, the soil should be in the best physical condition for crop growth and the soil surface is level. Land preparation involves ploughing and harrowing to 'till' or dig-up, mix and level the soil.

Tillage allows the seeds to be planted at the right depth, and also helps with weed control. Farmers can till the land themselves using hoes and other equipment or they can be assisted by draft animals, such as buffalo, or tractors and other machinery.

Next, the land is leveled to reduce the amount of water wasted by uneven pockets of too-deep water or exposed soil. Effective land leveling allows the seedlings to become established more easily, reduces the amount of effort required to manage the crop, and increases both grain quality and yields.

Harvesting is the process of collecting the mature rice crop from the field. Depending on the variety, a rice crop usually reaches maturity at around 105–150 days after crop establishment. Harvesting activities include cutting, stacking, handling, threshing, cleaning, and hauling. Good harvesting methods help maximize grain yield and minimize grain damage and deterioration.

Harvesting can be done manually or mechanically:

Manual harvesting is common across Asia It involves cutting the rice crop with simple hand tools like sickles and knives. Manual harvesting is very effective when a crop has lodged or fallen over, however it is labour intensive. Manual harvesting requires 40 to 80 hours per hectare and it takes additional labour to manually collect and haul the harvested crop.

Mechanical harvesting using reapers or combine harvesters is the other option, but not so common due to the availability and cost of machinery. Following cutting, the rice must be threshed to separate the grain from the stalk and cleaned. These processes can also be done by hand or machine.

What do these words and phrases from the text mean? Choose from the following list.

to get the highest amount,   preparation of the soil,   set firmly in position,   to put seed in the ground,   the action of preparing the soil,   a crop flattened by rain or wind,   breaking up the soil with a too which has teeth,   spikes or discs,   a small depression or cavity,   touching and moving something with the hands, turn up the earth before planting seeds,   to pull and drag with effort and force,   a wild plant growing where it is not wanted, to take things apart from each other,   a small young plant raised from a seed,   a motor vehicle used for pulling and dragging other farm machinery,   a large heavy animal,   when something is done very well,   to hit a plant hard to separate the seed,   to not use something well,   something used as a machine,   to divide into pieces uses a knife or a sharp instrument,   a grain used for planting so as to grow other plants,   not level,   an instrument for tilling / mixing / raking,   a curved knife used for cutting,   animals used on a farm for heavy work such as pulling and hauling,   a small dry seed,   using manpower more than machine power,   a decrease in the quality of something,   how good something is,   putting things in a pile / one on top of the other,   the long stem of a plant,   to give gain,   using the hands,   to make smaller,   a unit of measurement of land

1.) to plant _____

2.) ploughing _____

3.) harrowing _____

4.) till _____

5.) tillage _____

6.) seed _____

7.) weed _____

8.) hoe _____

9.) draft animal _____

10.) buffalo _____

11.) tractor _____

12.) uneven _____

13.) pocket _____

14.) waste _____

15.) seedlings_____

16.) established _____

17.) effort _____

18.) grain _____

19.) quality _____

20.)cutting _____

21.)stacking _____

22.)handling _____

23.)threshing _____

24.)hauling _____

25.)yield _____

26.)maximize _____

27.)minimize _____

28.)deterioration _____

29.)manual _____

30.)sickle _____

31.)mechanical _____

32.)effective _____

33.)lodged _____

34.)labour intensive _____

35.)hectare _____

36.)stalk _____

37.)separate _____

Answer the questions in complete sentences

1.) What should happen before rice is planted?

_____

_____

2.) What does land preparation involve?

_____

_____

3.) What does tillage allow?

_____

_____

4.) How can farmers till the land themselves?

_____

_____

5.) Why is the land levelled?

_____

_____

6.) What is harvesting?

_____

_____

7.) How long does it take for a rice crop to mature?

_____

_____

8.) What do harvesting activities include?

_____

_____

9.) What are the two ways harvesting can be done?

_____

_____

10.) Where is manual harvesting common?

_____

_____

Say if these sentences are true (T) or false (F)

1.) Tillage helps with weed control. _____

2.) Land levelling destroys the seedlings. _____

3.) Cutting, stacking, handling, threshing, cleaning are planting activities. _____

4.) The rice is threshed before cutting. _____

5.) Mechanical harvesting is more costly than manual harvesting. _____

Choose *a, b, c* or *d*

1.) Farmers can use _____for tillage.

a.) camels   b.) draft animals   c.) donkeys   d.) dogs

2.) Levelling the land increases _____.

a.) weeds   b.) water   c.) soil   d.) grain quality and yields.

3.) Manual harvesting involves cutting the rice crop with _____.

a.) machines   b.) tools   c.) draft animals   d.) weeds

4.) After cutting, the rice must be _____.

    a.) eaten b.) planted c.) threshed d.) tilled

5.) Threshing separates the grain from the _____.

    a.) stalk b.) weeds c.) rice d.) machines.

UNIT 4

Seventy kilometres from Muscat's city center is the coastal city of Barka. You can find the Pairidaeza farm which has10 acres of land. It is Oman's first and only organic farm.

Pairidaeza first began with Narjes Mirza's love for growing fresh organic agricultural produce for her family. She also wanted to provide chemical-free fruit and vegetables to all people who desired to eat healthy food.

As a result of her relentless efforts, Narjes received certification from the United States Department of Agriculture. She has got many other accolades too for her success in organic farming.

Narjes works with her daughters on the farm. Their hard work has transformed Pairidaeza into a local household name. Their farm now supplies produce to many large retail supermarkets in the country. "My very own family forms the core of this farm's operations. One of my daughters takes care of everything that has to do with seeds, another is looking after dairy production and yet another in overseeing the harvesting. Together, we make a very effective team in ensuring our products are up to standard and of the highest quality."

Although the concept of organic farming in Oman is still new, there has been an increase in demand for organic foods over the years. As the pioneer of organic farming in Oman, Narjes hopes that her local experience will inspire other farmers locally, regionally and globally.

What do these words and phrases from the text mean? Choose from the following list.

award, someone who is first to do something new, make sure, near the coast, work / activities, at a level which is acceptable, to continue without stopping / extremely determined, the very best available, centre / the most important, what customers are asking for, a government ministry which deals with agricultural issues, everywhere in the world, a unit of land measurement, supervise / manage, selling directly to the public, part of a country, a strong wish, encourage / cause people to become interested in something, popular / spoken about everywhere, a substance with no added chemicals, in the area nearby, a farm which does not use artificial or chemical fertilisers, milk based products, to change something completely, an idea, approval / validation, hard work

1.) coastal _____

2.) acre _____

3.) organic farm _____

4.) desire _____

5.) chemical-free _____

6.) relentless _____

7.) effort _____

8.) certification _____

9.) Department of Agriculture _____

10.) accolades _____

11.) transform _____

12.) household name _____

13.) retail _____

14.) core _____

15.) operations _____

16.) dairy _____

17.) oversee _____

18.) ensure _____

19.) up to standard _____

20.) highest quality _____

21.) concept _____

22.) demand _____

23.) pioneer _____

24.) inspire _____

25.) local _____

26.) region _____

27.) global _____

Answer the questions in complete sentences.

1.) How far is Barka from Muscat city centre?

_____

_____

2.) How many acres of land has the Pairidaeza farm got?

_____

_____

3.) How many organic farms are there in Oman?

_____

_____

4.) Who started the Pairidaeza farm?

_____

_____

5.) What did she have a love for?

_____

_____

6.) What did she want to provide?

_____

_____

7.) What did she receive from the US Department of Agriculture?

_____

_____

8.) Who does she work with on the farm?

_____

_____

9.) Where does the farm supply its produce to?

_____

_____

10.) What has the family's hard work transformed Pairidaeza farm into?

_____

_____

Say if these sentences are true (T) or false (F)

1.) Narjes Mizra started the farm. _____

2.) Her fruit and vegetables contain chemical additives. _____

3.) We can deduce from the text that Narjes has three daughters. _____

4.) The concept of organic farming in Oman is old. _____

5.) There has been no increase in demand for organic products in Oman. _____

Choose *a, b, c* or *d*

1.) Narjes Mizra started _____ farm.

a.) an inorganic   b.) an organic   c.) a poultry   d.) an urban

2.) At first, Narjes wanted to grow healthy food for her _____.

a.) family   b.) neighbours   c.) for export   d.) uncle

3.) She got accolades for her _____ in organic farming.

a.) failure   b.) love   c.) joy   d.) success

4.) Her _____ work on the farm.

a.) sons   b.) workers   c.) daughters   d.) animals

5.) Narjes is a _____in organic farming.

a.) pioneer   b.) labourer   c.) failure   d.) farm

UNIT 5
Subsistence Farming

Sub Saharan Africa. (Green colour)

What it is:

Subsistence farming or smallholder agriculture is when one family grows only enough to feed themselves. There is not usually much harvest to sell or trade, and what surplus there is, is usually stored to last the family until the next harvest. This is the most widely used method of agricultural farming in sub-Saharan Africa, and the majority of the rural poor depend on it for survival. It's a method that has appeal to rural farmers because it allows food to be produced (with very little cost) in the rural areas, it lessens their need to find transportation to a city, and it creates opportunity to continue living in a village (where housing and land are much more affordable). It also means the family is self-sufficient in terms of food. Ideally, nothing needs to be purchased or borrowed from another source.

Why it doesn't work:

For one, it is very susceptible to climate change. If there is a drought, if there is a flood, the harvest is severely limited that year. This means there might actually *not* be enough to feed the family. Subsistence farming works when everything goes right – but it rarely does. And even then, there is no profit generated. There's no way to make money off of the farm, meaning that the family works to grow their food, but they lose time that could have been spent working for income. Subsistence farming is a deterrent to development in rural Africa, because it has no possible upward movement. Unless it switches to a semi-commercial model it will continue to prevent people from generating income.

What do these words and phrases from the text mean? Choose from the following list.

a system / a method,   attracting,   when the land is parched because of no rain,   to change,   extra above one's basic needs,   when a person can meet all his / her needs without reliance on other sources,   bought,   progression,   money from salary or profits,   in the countryside / outside of a town or city,   too much water because of too much rain,   half, money remaining after all expenses have been paid,   lorries, buses,   cars etc,   seldom,   to rely on,   to make / create, to continue in existence,   prone to / to be vulnerable to,   to reduce,   to discourage someone from doing something,   a beginning,   at a reasonable price where most people have enough money to buy it

1.) surplus _____

2.) rural _____

3.) depend _____

4.) survival _____

5.) appeal _____

6.) lessen _____

7.) transportation _____

8.) affordable _____

9.) self- sufficient _____

10.) purchased _____

11.) source _____

12.) susceptible _____

13.) drought _____

14.) flood _____

15.) profit _____

16.) generate _____

17.) rarely _____

18.) income _____

19.) deterrent _____

20.) switch _____

21.) semi _____

22.) model _____

23.) upward movement _____

Answer the questions in complete sentences.

1.) What is another name for subsistence farming?

_____

_____

2.) What is subsistence farming?

_____

_____

3.) Where is subsistence farming the most widely used form of agriculture?

_____

_____

4.) Why does it appeal to rural farmers?

_____

_____

5.) What is subsistence farming susceptible to?

_____

_____

6.) What two things can limit the harvest in any particular year?

_____

_____

7.) When does subsistence farming work?

_____

_____

8.) What is subsistence farming a deterrent to in rural Africa?

_____

_____

9.) Why is it a deterrent?

_____

_____

10.) How can subsistence farming generate more income?

_____

_____

Say if these sentences are true (T) or false (F)

1.) Subsistence farming produces large surpluses. _____

2.) A minority of rural poor depend on subsistence farming. _____

3.) In an ideal situation, nothing needs to be purchased or borrowed from another source. _____

4.) In droughts or floods, subsistence farmers may not be able to produce enough to meet their families' needs. _____

5.) Subsistence farming has upward movement potential._____

Choose *a, b, c* or *d*

1.) In subsistence farming there is _____ not much surplus to trade or sell.

   a.) always   b.) often   c.) usually   d.) sometimes

2.) Subsistence farming is widely used in _____Africa.

   a.) northern   b.) southern   c.) eastern and western   d.) sub-Saharan

3.) In a drought or flood, there is _____to feed the family.

   a.) not enough   b.) enough   c.) plenty   d.) sufficient

4.) Subsistence farmers have insufficient time to work for _____.

   a.) the harvest   b.) income   c.) produce   d.) agriculture.

5.) In subsistence farming things _____go right.

   a.) often   b.) never   c.) sometimes   d.) rarely

READING FOR ENJOYMENT
Stonehenge

Sign up for the Inside History newsletter

- **SHOWSTHIS DAY IN HISTO**
  UPDATED:
  FEB 3, 2020
  ORIGINAL:
  FEB 21, 2019

Stonehenge

HISTORY.COM EDITORS

For centuries, historians and archaeologists have wondered about the many mysteries of Stonehenge, the prehistoric monument that took Neolithic builders an estimated 1,500 years to erect. Located in southern England, it is comprised of roughly 100 massive upright stones placed in a circular layout.

While many modern scholars now agree that Stonehenge was once a burial ground, they have not discovered what other purposes it served and how a civilization without modern technology—or even the wheel—produced the mighty monument. Its construction is all the more baffling because, while the sandstone slabs of its outer ring hail from local quarries, scientists have traced the bluestones that make up its inner ring all the way to the Preseli Hills in Wales, some 200 miles from where Stonehenge sits on Salisbury Plain. It is a mystery how such people who did not have the wheel transported these huge stones all the way to Salisbury Plain.

Nearly 1 million people every year visit Stonehenge, a UNESCO World Heritage Site since 1986.

Answer the following questions.

1.) What have historians and archeologists wondered about for centuries?

_____

_____

2.) Who built Stonehenge?

_____

_____

3.) How long did it take them to build Stonehenge?

_____

_____

4.) Where is Stonehenge located?

_____

_____

5.) How many stones is it comprised of?

_____

_____

6.) Where do the sandstone slabs of its outer ring come from?

_____

_____

7.) How far are Stonehenge and the Preseli Hills from each other?

_____

_____

8.) On which plain does Stonehenge sit?

_____

_____

9.) How many people visit Stonehenge every year?

_____

_____

10.) When did Stonehenge become a UNESCO World Heritage Site?

_____

_____

THEME 13

NATURAL PHENOMENA

UNIT 1
Rain

You need clouds to make rain. Clouds form from water or ice that has evaporated from the Earth's surface, or from plants that give off water and oxygen as a product of photosynthesis. When it evaporates—that is, rises from Earth's surface into the atmosphere—water is in the form of a gas. This gas is called water vapour. Water vapour turns into clouds when it cools and condenses—that is, turns back into liquid water or ice. In order to condense, the water vapour must have a solid to glom onto. This solid "seed" may be a speck of dust or pollen, or a drop of water or crystal of ice. Dew is water vapor that has condensed back onto Earth's surface—on grass or a car's windshield, for example.

In the cloud, with more water condensing onto other water droplets, the droplets grow. When they get too heavy to stay suspended in the cloud, even with updrafts within the cloud, they fall to Earth as rain. If the air in the cloud is below the freezing point (32 °F or 0 °C), ice crystals form; if the air all the way down to the ground is also freezing, or below freezing, you get snow. However, if the layers of atmosphere within the cloud, and between the cloud and the ground, alternate between warmer than freezing and colder than freezing, you get other kinds of precipitation.

What do these words and phrases from the text mean? Choose from the following list.

to stick on / become attached to,   to make,   a very tiny spot, to change from a gas to a liquid,   repeated change between two contrasting conditions,   the process by which green plants and some other organisms use sunlight to make nutrients from carbon dioxide and water,   an upward movement of air,   to change from a liquid into a gas,   a very fine powder,   a solid with patterns on it,   the outside or uppermost part of something,   strong / not a liquid or a gas,   the front window of a car,   something from the male part of the flower,   one of several coverings over a surface and arranged one on top of the other,   a very small drop of a liquid,   very short green plants,   something that flows freely – like water,   product of the condensation of atmospheric water vapor that falls under gravitational pull from clouds,   hanging in the air / not falling to the ground

1.) evaporate _____

2.) surface _____

3.) photosynthesis _____

4.) condense _____

5.) glom _____

6.) crystal _____

7.) windshield _____

8.) droplet _____

9.) suspend _____

10.) updraft _____

11.) solid _____

12.) grass _____

13.) layer _____

14.) alternate _____

15.) precipitation _____

16.) liquid _____

17.) suspend _____

18.) speck _____

19.) dust _____

20.) pollen _____

Answer the questions in complete sentences

1.) What do you need to make rain?

_____

_____

2.) From where do clouds form?

_____

_____

3.) What do plants give off as a product of photosynthesis?

_____

_____

4.) When water evaporates from the surface of the Earth, where does it go?

_____

_____

5.) What is the name of this gas?

_____

_____

6.) What happens to water vapour when it cools and condenses?

_____

_____

7.) What must the water vapour have in order to condense?

_____

_____

8.) What is dew?

_____

_____

9.) What happens when the water droplets get too heavy?

_____

_____

10.) What happens if the air in the cloud is below freezing point?

_____

_____

Say if these sentences are true (T) or false (F)

1.) Droplets grow when more water condenses onto other water droplets. _____

2.) Thirty two degrees centigrade is below freezing point. _____

3.) If the air all the way down to the ground is freezing, you get more rain. _____

4.) The picture shows the water cycle. _____

5.) There is no precipitation if the layers of atmosphere within the cloud alternate between warming and freezing. _____

Choose *a, b, c* or *d*

1.) Plants give off _____ when they photosynthesise.

a.) water and nitrogen   b.) methane and ethane   c.) water and oxygen   d.) helium and hydrogen

2.) Evaporating water rises in the _____.

a.) atmosphere   b.) plants   c.) cycle   d.) oxygen

3.) The Fahrenheit freezing point is _____ degrees.

a.) 13   b.) 23   c.) 0   d.) 32

4.) The water cycle picture shows water storage in the _____.

a.) clouds   b.) oceans   c.) plants   d.) rain

5.) The _____ seed in the droplet may be a speck of dust or pollen.

a.) liquid   b.) gas   c.) solid   d.) snow

UNIT 2
Earthquakes

An earthquake is caused by a sudden slip on a fault. The tectonic plates are always slowly moving, but they get stuck at their edges due to friction. When the stress on the edge overcomes the friction, there is an earthquake that releases energy in waves that travel through the earth's crust and cause the shaking that we feel. **Tectonic plates** are pieces of Earth's crust. The **plates** are around 100 km (62 miles) thick and consist of two principal types of material: oceanic crust (also called sima from silicon and magnesium) and continental crust (sial from silicon and aluminium).

In California there are two plates - the Pacific Plate and the North American Plate. The Pacific Plate consists of most of the Pacific Ocean floor and the California Coast line. The North American Plate comprises most the North American Continent and parts of the Atlantic Ocean floor. The primary boundary between these two plates is the San Andreas Fault. The San Andreas Fault is more than 650 miles long and extends to depths of at least 10 miles. Many other smaller faults like the Hayward (Northern California) and the San Jacinto (Southern California) branch from and join the San Andreas Fault Zone.

The Pacific Plate grinds northwestward past the North American Plate at a rate of about two inches per year. Parts of the San Andreas Fault system adapt to this movement by constant "creep" resulting in many tiny shocks and a few moderate earth tremors. In other areas where creep is NOT constant, strain can build up for hundreds of years, producing great earthquakes when it finally releases.

What do these words and phrases from the text mean? Choose from the following list.

to move very slowly, the furthest point of a thing or place, to be formed of / to be made up of, to let go of something / to free someone or something, a boundary between two tectonic plates, pressure or tension on a material object, to cover a wider area / make larger, power, pull / push / stretch something with a lot of force, accumulate, slide quickly over a short distance, a periodic variation of an electromagnetic field, pieces of the Earth's crust that move, not too much or too little of something, rapid up and down or side to side movements, an object fixed in a tight position and it is very difficult to get it out of that position, the main thing / the most important, to extend outwards from a main source, a very small earthquake, the action of one surface or object rubbing hard against another, a violent shaking movement, the distance between the top of a surface and the bottom,   to succeed in solving a problem or a difficult situation,   the top part of the layers of materials that the Earth is composed of,   to remain unchanged

1.) fault _____

2.) slip _____

3.) tectonic plates _____

4.) stuck _____

5.) edge _____

6.) friction _____

7.) stress _____

8.) overcome _____

9.) release _____

10.) energy _____

11.) wave _____

12.) the Earth's crust _____

13.) shake _____

14.) consist / comprise _____

15.) primary / principle _____

16.) extend _____

17.) depth _____

18.) branch from _____

19.) grind / creep_____

20.)shocks _____

21.) moderate _____

22.)earth tremors _____

23.)constant _____

24.)strain _____

25.)build up _____

Answer the questions in complete sentences

1.) What is an earthquake caused by?

_____

_____

2.) What are the tectonic plates doing?

_____

_____

3.) What causes the tectonic plates to get stuck?

_____

_____

4.) When is there an earthquake?

_____

_____

5.) How thick are the tectonic plates?

_____

_____

6.) How many plates are there in California?

_____

_____

7.) Where does the Pacific Plate grind?

_____

_____

8.) What is the rate of grind of the Pacific Plate?

_____

_____

9.) How do parts of the San Andreas Fault system adapt to this movement?

_____

_____

10.) How long can strain build up for in areas where creep is not constant?

_____

_____

Say if these sentences are true (T) or false (F)

1.) Tectonic plates get stuck at their edges due to water. _____

2.) An earthquake releases energy in straight lines. _____

3.) The oceanic crust contains silver and magnesium. _____

4.) The Pacific Plate consists of most of the Atlantic Ocean floor. _____

5.) The San Andreas Fault is more than 650 miles long. _____

Choose *a, b, c* or *d*

1.) The continental crust contains _____.

a.) silicon and gold   b.) gold and silver   c.) aluminium and iron   d.) aluminium and silicon

2.) The Pacific Plate and the North American Plate are in _____.

a.) California   b.) New York   c.) Texas   d.) Idaho

3.) The San Andreas Fault is at least _____ deep.

a.) ten kilometers   b.) ten feet   c.) ten miles   d.) 10 metres

4.) The San Andreas Fault is the main _____between the Pacific Plate and the North American plate.

a.) plate   b.) boundary   c.) silicon   d.) fault

5.) Tiny shocks and moderate earth tremors are caused by _____.

a.) earthquakes   b.) California   c.) aluminium   d.) creep

UNIT 3
Volcanoes

Attila Kilinc, head of the geology department at the University of Cincinnati, answers the question – How do volcanoes erupt? Most recently, Professor Kilinc has been studying volcanoes in Hawaii and Montserrat.

When a part of the earth's upper mantle or lower crust melts, magma forms. A volcano is essentially an opening or a vent through which this magma and the dissolved gases it contains are discharged. Although there are several factors triggering a volcanic eruption, three predominate: the buoyancy of the magma, the pressure from the exsolved gases in the magma and the injection of a new batch of magma into an already filled magma chamber.

Lighter magma rises toward the surface because of its buoyancy. If the density of the magma between the area where it is made and the surface is less than that of the surrounding rocks, the magma reaches the surface and erupts.

Although volcanologists are well aware of these processes, they cannot predict a volcanic eruption. But they can look at the history of certain volcanoes. By understanding the past behaviour of a volcano, they can predict that the volcano will do the same again in the future.

What do these words and phrases from the text mean? Choose from the following list.

to cause something to happen, arrive at a place, molten rock material within the earth, to say what will happen in the future, to forcefully put something into something else, the study of rocks, to separate from a solid substance, to apply strong force on something, the ability of something to float in a liquid, a scientist who studies volcanoes, to make a solid break up in a fluid, the distribution of something over a unit of measurement, when a substance comes out from a confined area, around something / circling something, a natural or artificial enclosed space, to suddenly come out from an enclosed area, to change from a solid to a liquid due to heat, a group, most importantly, a thing that helps a result happen, most influential / have the advantage

1.) geology _____

2.) erupt _____

3.) melt _____

4.) magma _____

5.) essentially _____

6.) dissolve _____

7.) discharge _____

8.) factor _____

9.) trigger _____

10.) predominate _____

11.) buoyancy _____

12.) pressure _____

13.) exsolve _____

14.) injection _____

15.) batch _____

16.) chamber _____

17.) density _____

18.) surrounding _____

19.) reach _____

20.) vulcanologist _____

21.) predict _____

Answer the questions in complete sentences

1.) Who is Attila Kilnic?

_____

_____

2.) What question does he answer?

_____

_____

3.) Where has he been studying volcanoes?

_____

_____

4.) How does magma form?

_____

_____

5.) What essentially is a volcano?

_____

_____

6.) How many factors predominate in the triggering of a volcanic eruption?

_____

_____

7.) Why does lighter magma rise towards the surface?

_____

_____

8.) What are volcanologists aware of?

_____

_____

9.) What can't they predict?

_____

_____

10.) What can they look at?

_____

_____

Say if these sentences are true (T) or false (F)

1.) Attila Kilnic works at the University of Cincinnati. _____

2.) A vent is different from an opening. _____

3.) Several factors are involved in triggering a volcanic eruption. _____

4.) The magma erupts under the surface. _____

5.) Volcanologists can easily predict a volcanic eruption. _____

Choose *a, b, c* or *d*

1.) Attila Kilnic is _____.

a.) a teacher   b.) a professor   c.) a student   d.) an historian

2.) The _____of the Earth is between the crust and the outer core.

  a.) core   b.) inner core   c.) mantle   d.) volcano

3.) The _____is at the centre of the Earth.

  a.) core   b.) crust   c.) mantle   d.) inner core

4.) The outer core is _____thick.

  a.) 8 – 10 km   b.) 2,000 km   c.) 2,250 km   d.) 1,000 km

5.) The _____ is the thinnest part of the Earth's structure.

  a.) mantle   b.) core   c.) crust   d.) outer core

UNIT 4
Mountains

There are a few ways that mountains can form. One thing these methods have in common is that they all take millions of years!

Most mountains formed from Earth's tectonic plates smashing together. Below the ground, the Earth's crust is made up of multiple tectonic plates. They've been moving around since the beginning of time. And they still move today as a result of geologic activity below the surface. On average, these plates move at a rate of about one to two inches each year.

When two tectonic plates come together, their edges can crumple. Think of what happens to a pepsi can when you crush it. It's a bit like that! The result of these tectonic plates crumpling is huge slabs of rock being pushed up into the air. What are those called? Mountains, of course! Specifically, these are called "fold mountains."

For example, the tectonic plates that lie underneath India and Asia crashed into each other over 25 million years ago. What happened? The Himalayas, including Mount Everest, formed. And they're still pushing against each other. That means the Himalayas are still growing even today!

Sometimes, instead of crashing together, two tectonic plates grind against each other. Occasionally, this results in one plate lifting up and tilting over. The result? A fault-block mountain range! One example is the Sierra Nevada mountain range in California.

Other times, a unique type of mountain is made when one plate is pushed below the other, pushing magma to the surface. This is how volcanoes, like Mount Fuji, are made. Volcanic activity below Earth's surface can also result in new mountains when magma is pushed up toward the surface. When that happens, it cools and forms hard rock. The result is dome mountains.

What do these words and phrases from the text mean? Choose from the following list.

nothing else like it / the only one,   when two or more things hit each other violently at high speed,   more exactly,   many,   to damage something in a way that makes it creased and wrinkled, a lot of mountains all very close together,   to damage something by compressing it and squeezing it forcefully,   something moving at a sloping position,   a large,   thick,   flat piece of stone or concrete,   usually square or rectangular in shape

1.) smash /crash _____

2.) crush _____

3.) crumple _____

4.) slab _____

5.) specifically _____

6.) tilt _____

7.) mountain range _____

8.) unique _____

9.) multiple _____

Answer the questions in complete sentences

1.) How long does it take for mountains to form?

_____

_____

2.) How were most mountains formed?

_____

_____

3.) What is the Earth's crust made of?

_____

_____

4.) How far do tectonic plates move every year?

_____

_____

5.) What happens when two tectonic plates come together?

_____

_____

6.) How long did it take for the Himalayas and Mount Everest to form?

_____

_____

7.) What kind of mountain range is formed when two tectonic plates grind against each other?

_____

_____

8.) Where is the Sierra Nevada mountain range?

_____

_____

9.) What kind of mountain is formed when one plate is pushed below the other?

_____

_____

10.) What kind of mountains are formed when magma is pushed up towards the surface and cooled?

_____

_____

Say if these sentences are true (T) or false (F)

1.) Mountains can form in only one way. _____

2.) The Himalayas are in India and Asia. _____

3.) The Himalayas are still getting taller today. _____

4.) A fault-block mountain range is formed by two tectonic plates grinding against each other. _____

5.) Mount Fuji is a fold mountain. _____

Choose *a, b, c* or *d*

1.) The Earth's crust is _____.

    a.) above ground b.) in a mountain c.) below ground
    d.) near volcanoes

2.) Tectonic plates _____.

    a.) are still moving today b.) have stopped moving today
    c.) move very far and fast d.) do not now exist

3.) Huge slabs of _____are pushed into the air when two tectonic plates' edges crumple.

    a.) magma b.) rock c.) stones d.) crust

4.) Volcanoes are _____mountains.

    a.) common b.) crust c.) unique d.) tectonic

5.) Dome mountains are made of _____.

    a.) slabs b.) tectonic plates c.) magma d.) dust

UNIT 5
Stars

The twinkling lights in the sky are stars. Our own sun is a star. Sometimes we think that all those stars are the same. In fact, there are many types of stars, and we can see most of these in the night sky.

Solar-type Stars

A solar-type star has about the same mass as our Sun and is fusing hydrogen into helium at its core. The result is the familiar yellow glow that we see on many of the stars we look at in the sky. Stars like our sun have a lifetime of billions of years.

Hot Blue Stars

Stars which are much more massive than our Sun burn hotter but for much less time, living and dying within a few million years. These stars show a bright blue light because they are very hot. And because they're so bright, we can see a lot of them from the ground without having to use binoculars or a telescope.

Red Dwarf Stars

Stars which are much less massive than our Sun burn cooler and live longer – potentially for hundreds of billions of years. The resulting dull red stars are actually the most common type in our galaxy but since they're quite dim, they're hard to see.

Red Giant Stars

When a star runs out of hydrogen fuel in its core, it has to adjust and find alternative ways to power itself – one of the ways it does this is to start burning hydrogen outside the core and this makes the star swell up. The result is a cool, red giant star. Because these stars are so large, they are bright, and we can see several in our skies.

White Dwarfs

When a star about the size of our Sun, or a little larger, has burnt all the material it can, it collapses into a white dwarf. This is a very small star – only about the same size as planet Earth. It is very hot but very faint. Since these stars are so small and emit a lot of their light in the ultraviolet they can be very hard to see in our skies.

What do these words and phrases from the text mean? Choose from the following list.

possessing a strong possibility,   become large and bloated by outward extension,   the rapid change in the brightness of a star,   someone or something you know / not the first time you have seen someone or something,   produce and discharge something – especially gas or radiation,   fall suddenly and completely,   an optical instrument with a lens for one eye and used for viewing distant objects,   of a light which is not very strong / not bright,   to modify / to make a slight change, concerning the sun,   a type of light that is not visible to the human eye,   a round object that orbits the sun or a star, joining two things together usually by heat or some other type of energy source – like nuclear,   not shining brightly and difficult to see,   to give out a steady light without a flame,   to produce flames and heat while consuming a material,   an optical instrument with a lens for each eye and used for viewing distant objects,   when there is no more of something / when certain things have been all used,   another possibility or choice,

1.) twinkle _____

2.) solar _____

3.) fusion _____

4.) glow _____

5.) familiar _____

6.) binoculars _____

7.) dull / dim _____

8.) potentially _____

9.) runs out of _____

10.) adjust _____

11.) alternative _____

12.) swell _____

13.) burn _____

14.) collapse _____

15.) planet _____

16.) faint _____

17.) emit _____

18.) ultraviolet _____

19.) telescope _____

Answer the questions in complete sentences

1.) What is our own sun?

_____

_____

2.) What are solar-type stars?

_____

_____

3.) Where does the sun fuse hydrogen into helium?

_____

_____

4.) How long do stars like our sun live for?

_____

_____

5.) Which stars are more massive and hotter than our sun?

_____

_____

6.) Why do these stars show a bright blue light?

_____

_____

7.) Why are red dwarf stars hard to see?

_____

_____

8.) What makes red giant stars swell up?

_____

_____

9.) What do stars like our sun collapse into?

_____

_____

10.) What kind of light do white dwarfs emit?

_____

_____

Say if these sentences are true (T) or false (F)

1.) Stars are other suns. _____

2.) Stars twinkle. _____

3.) Our sun is a hot blue star. _____

4.) A red dwarf is a massive star. _____

5.) It is hard to see a white dwarf. _____

Choose *a, b, c* or *d*

1.) Solar type stars fuse hydrogen into _____.

   a.) methane   b.) ethane   c.) nitrogen   d.) helium

2.) Solar type stars are _____.

   a.) yellow   b.) blue   c.) red   d.) orange

3.) To see stars close up, we use _____.

   a.) ultraviolet light   b.) helium   c.) binoculars or a telescope
   d.) hydrogen

4.) The Earth is a _____.

   a.) star   b.) planet   c.) sun   d.) red dwarf

5.) Stars less massive than our sun have potential lives of
   _____ of years.

   a.) hundreds of thousands   b.) hundreds of millions
   c.) hundreds and hundreds   d.) hundreds of billions

READING FOR ENJOYMENT
The National Museum of Oman

The National Museum is considered to be a vital project. It aims to achieve a cultural and humanitarian mission. It desires to raise public awareness, and cement Omani noble values. Furthermore, it has the hope of increasing Omani people's awareness, of their history, heritage, and culture. The ultimate goal is to advance their creative and intellectual abilities.

ArCHIAM was invited to contribute to the exhibitions both with presentation material (drawings, still images and animations), the curation of parts of the galleries and the development of contents for incorporation into touch screens.

As a national institution with global outreach, the National Museum is dedicated to ensuring Oman's cultural heritage is understood and appreciated not only within the Sultanate, but also internationally. Furthermore, it aims to provide opportunities for cultural expression and innovation. It is also working towards achieving the transfer of traditional skills and knowledge from one generation to the next. It is also the first public building in the Sultanate that includes advanced facilities for disabled people, including exhibits with Arabic Braille captions.

Answer the questions in complete sentences

1.) What is considered to be a vital project?

_____

_____

2.) Which organization was invited to contribute to the exhibition?

_____

_____

3.) What kind of mission does the museum aim to achieve?

_____

_____

4.) What is the museum's desire?

_____

_____

5.) Which three things does the museum hope to increase?

_____

_____

6.) What is the museum's ultimate goal?

_____

_____

7.) What kind of outreach does the National Museum have?

_____

_____

8.) What does the museum aim to provide?

_____

_____

9.) What is it working towards achieving?

_____

_____

10.) What two facilities does the museum provide for disabled people?

_____

_____

THEME 14

BREAKTHROUGHS

UNIT 1
Thomas Edison

Edison was born on February 11, 1847, in Milan, Ohio. He was the youngest of seven children of Samuel and Nancy Edison. He was America's greatest inventor. Here are a few of the most notable inventions of Edison.

In December 1877, Edison developed a method for recording sound: the phonograph. His innovation relied upon tin cylinders with two needles: one for recording sound, and another for playback.

His first words spoken into the phonograph's mouthpiece were, "Mary had a little lamb." Though not commercially viable for another decade, the phonograph brought him worldwide fame, especially when the device was used by the U.S. Army to bring music to the troops overseas during World War I.

While Edison was not the inventor of the first light bulb, he came up with the technology that helped bring it to the masses.

In 1887, Edison built an industrial research laboratory in West Orange, New Jersey, which served as the primary research laboratory for the Edison lighting companies.

He spent most of his time there, supervising the development of lighting technology and power systems. He also perfected the phonograph and developed the motion picture camera and the alkaline storage battery.

On April 23, 1896, Edison became the first person to project a motion picture, showing the world's first motion picture at Koster & Bial's Music Hall in New York City.

His interest in motion pictures began years earlier, when he and an associate named W. K. L. Dickson developed a Kinetoscope, a viewing device. Soon, Edison's West Orange laboratory was creating Edison Films. Among the first of these was *The Great Train Robbery*, released in 1903.

What do these words and phrases from the text mean? Choose from the following list.

a shape which is longer than it is wide, abroad / in another country, remarkable / worthy of attention, the first / the most important, a partner / a co-worker, an extremely thin and sharp piece of metal used to play records, ready for sale on the open market, a type of primary battery that obtains its energy from the reaction between zinc metal and manganese dioxide, depend upon, soldiers, the multitudes, a kind of metal

1.) notable _____

2.) rely _____

3.) tin _____

4.) cylinder _____

5.) needle _____

6.) troops _____

7.) overseas _____

8.) the masses _____

9.) primary _____

10.) supervise _____

11.) alkaline battery _____

12.) an associate _____

13.) commercially viable _____

Answer these questions in complete sentences.

1.) When was Thomas Edison born?

_____

_____

2.) How many children were there in his family?

_____

_____

3.) What is a phonograph?

_____

_____

4.) What words did Edison speak into the phonograph?

_____

_____

5.) What did the US army use the phonograph for?

_____

_____

6.) Who was Edison's lighting technology brought to?

_____

_____

7.) Where did Edison build an industrial research laboratory?

_____

_____

8.) What did he perfect?

_____

_____

9.) What did he develop?

_____

_____

10.) Who was Edison's associate?

_____

_____

Choose *a, b, c* or *d*.

1.) Edison was America's _____ inventor.

a.) great   b.) greater   c.) the great   d.) greatest

2.) Edison _____ many things in his lifetime.

a.) developed   b.) develops   c.) develop   d.) developing

3.) The phonograph _____ Edison great fame throughout the world.

   a.) bring b.) brought c.) brings d.) bringing

4.) Edison _____ the first person to project a moving picture.

   a.) become b.) became c.) becoming d.) becomes

5.) Edison's first film _____ *The Great Train Robbery.*

   a.) is b.) were c.) was d.) are

Say if these sentences are true (T) or false (F)

1.) Edison developed a method for recording motion pictures in 1877. _____

2.) The cylinders were made of tin. _____

3.) Edison's phonograph went on sale in 1887. _____

4.) Edison built an industrial research laboratory in 1877. _____

5.) His device for viewing motion pictures was called a Kinetoscope. _____

UNIT 2
Michael Faraday

Michael Faraday was a British scientist who lived from September 22, 1791, to August 25, 1867. Faraday is famous for discoveries in electromagnetism and electrochemistry. Because of his discoveries, he is often called the Father of Electricity. Michael Faraday's inventions ultimately changed the world and led to many technologies used today.

.Many also consider him the Father of Electromagnetism. This is because Faraday discovered electromagnetic induction, and he found a way to convert magnetic force into electrical force. Faraday's work would go on to inspire others to follow in his footsteps, forever changing the world.

In fact, Faraday's first known experiment was a chemistry experiment in which he decomposed magnesium sulfate. He also worked on improving steel alloys. In 1823, Faraday liquefied chlorine gas for the first time. In 1825, he discovered bicarburet of hydrogen, now known as benzene.

Faraday made a number of scientific discoveries that led to both his own inventions, and to many other technological innovations over time. Michael Faraday's inventions include the transformer, the electric motor, and the electric dynamo or generator.

The electric power used around the world relies upon Faraday's discoveries and inventions almost two centuries ago. All energy sources still rely on a generator to produce the electrical current that powers everything people use. The next time you see a hydroelectric dam or a steam plant, remember the contributions of Michael Faraday.

What do these words and phrases from the text mean? Choose from the following list.

to do what someone else has done,   electricity made by water power,   interaction that occurs between electrically charged particles,   finally,   what is given as part of a whole,   to take followers in a direction,   a chemical compound consisting of salt and magnesium,   chemical reactions that involve electrical currents that converts the heat energy of steam into mechanical energy,   a device that transfers electric energy from one alternating-current circuit to one or more other circuits,   a metal composed of two or more elements,   reservoirs for water,   the production of an electromotive force across an electrical conductor in a changing magnetic field,   a system that converts

the heat energy of steam into mechanical energy,   to change
from one thing into another thing,   breaking down a compound
into simpler elements

1.) electromagnetism _____

2.) electrochemistry _____

3.) ultimately _____

4.) lead (past tense – led) _____

5.) electromagnetic induction _____

6.) convert _____

7.) follow in someone's footsteps _____

8.) transformer _____

9.) decompose _____

10.) magnesium sulfate _____

11.) alloy _____

12.) hydroelectric _____

13.) dam _____

14.) steam plant _____

15.) contribution _____

Answer these questions in complete sentences.

1.) What nationality was Michael Faraday?

_____

_____

2.) When was he born?

_____

_____

3.) When did he die?

_____

_____

4.) In what areas were his discoveries?

_____

_____

5.) What is Michael Faraday often called?

_____

_____

6.) What did he convert magnetic force into?

_____

_____

7.) What did Faraday do in 1823?

_____

_____

8.) What was benzene first known as?

_____

_____

9.) How long ago were Faraday's discoveries and inventions made?

_____

_____

10.) What do all energy sources rely on to produce electricity?

_____

_____

Choose *a, b, c* or *d*.

1.) Faraday _____ in 1867.

   a.) die   b.) dies   c.) died   d.) dying

2.) Faraday's _____ changed the world.

   a.) inventions   b.) inventors   c.) inventor   d.) invents

3.) Faraday _____ electromagnetic induction.

   a.) discover   b.) discovers   c.) discovering   d.) discovered

4.) He worked _____ improving steel alloys.

   a.) on   b.) by   c.) in   d.) to

5.) Faraday _____ a number of scientific discoveries.

   a.) makes   b.) makings   c.) make   d.) made

Say if these sentences are true (T) or false (F)

1.) Faradays is considered the Father of Electromagnetism.

_____

2.) Faraday invented electricity. _____

3.) Faraday liquefied chlorine gas in 1824. _____

4.) Faraday invented the electric car. _____

5.) Faraday invented the electric dynamo. _____

UNIT 3
The Miner's Safety Lamp

The miner's safety lamp is, one of the most important inventions of the nineteenth century. At the time of the industrial revolution coal replaced wood as the most important fuel for the new industries and cities. As the industrial revolution began to gather pace in the early 1800s, the demand for coal to fuel steam-powered machines, trains, ships and, later, the blast furnaces of the iron and steel industry, grew at a rapid rate. Coal mines opened across Britain – particularly in South Wales, Scotland and Central and Northern England.

A lamp that could light the way down the mines, without causing a disastrous explosion, was as essential.

Mining was exhausting, dirty and, dangerous work. One of the biggest hazards was firedamp – the name given to the collection of explosive gases that lay in between the layers of coal. In the early 1800s, miners used candles to light their way. Unsurprisingly, explosions were very common, as the gases were released and ignited by the naked flames. One of the worst of these mining disasters occurred near Newcastle-upon-Tyne, in May 1812, killing 92 miners. Something needed to be done. In 1815, two inventors, George Stephenson and Sir Humphry Davy each had individual ideas and designs for a safety lamp.

Stephenson's oil lamp sucked air into a tall, glass chimney. When firedamp entered the chimney, the oxygen was diluted, and the flame was extinguished. Any gases leaving the chimney had a very low amount of oxygen, which prevented the enclosed flame escaping into the atmosphere. Davy's design worked in a similar way but had a fine brass gauze meshed cylinder enclosing the flame. This gave less light than Stephenson's glass tube but was more robust. While neither design was perfect, both were a vast improvement on the naked flame.

Stephenson later used Davy's gauze as he revised and improved his own design. This would become the 'Geordie Lamp' which was used in mines in the North East of England for much of the nineteenth century. The safety lamp continued to evolve until the electric cap lamp began to take over in the twentieth century.

What do these words and phrases from the text mean? Choose from the following list.

to pull something inwards by a backward motion of the air, replace, a net type design – with small hole openings, to get better and improve, a furnace in which combustion is forced by a current of air under pressure, contained within bounds, a large-scale, rapid, or spectacular expansion or bursting out or forth, a historical time when there was a sudden appearance of industries and machine production, a long thin escape tube for smoke / gas /fumes, a strongly woven fabric of metal filaments, to speed up / quicken, an alloy consisting mainly of copper and zinc, a large amount, strong, to diminish the strength of something, the glowing gaseous part of a fire, something lying on top of another,

1.) industrial Revolution _____

2.) to gather pace _____

3.) blast furnace _____

4.) explosion _____

5.) layer _____

6.) chimney _____

7.) suck into _____

8.) dilute _____

9.) brass _____

10.) gauze _____

11.) mesh _____

12.) robust _____

13.) flame _____

14.) enclose _____

15.) take over _____

16.) vast _____

17.) evolve _____

Answer these questions in complete sentences.

1.) What is one of the most important inventions of the 19th century?

_____

_____

2.) What was the most important fuel for the new industries and cities?

_____

_____

3.) In which parts of Britain did coal mines manly open?

_____

_____

4.) What was essential in the mines?

_____

_____

5.) What was firedamp?

_____

_____

6.) How many miners died in the explosion in the coal mine in Newcastle-upon-Tyne in 1812?

_____

_____

7.) Who had ideas about a safety lamp for miners?

_____

_____

8.) What did Stephenson later use?

_____

_____

9.) Where was the Geordie Lamp used?

_____

_____

10.) What lamp was used in the 20th century?

_____

_____

Choose *a, b, c* or *d*.

1.) The industrial revolution _____pace in the 19ᵗʰ century.

   a.) gather   b.) gathering   c.) gathered   d.) to gather

2.) The lamp lit the way _____the mines.

   a.) down   b.) on   c.) above   d.) near

3.) Mining was an _____ job.

   a.) exhaust   b.) exhausted   c.) exhausts   d.) exhausting

4.) There _____ a mining disaster in Newcastle-upon-Tyne in 1812.

   a.) is   b.) were   c.) was   d.) are

5.) The safety lamp _____throughout the 19ᵗʰ century.

   a.) evolve   b.) to evolve   c.) evolving   d.) evolved

Say if these sentences are true (T) or false (F)

1.) Coal was used before wood. _____

2.) Firedamp was a danger to miners. _____

3.) Davy's lamp worked in a dissimilar way to Stephenson's lamp. _____

4.) Davy's and Stephenson's lamps were perfect. _____

5.) Davy's and Stephenson's lamps were replaced in the 20ᵗʰ century. _____

UNIT 4
Hassan Kamel Assabbah

Hassan Kamel Assabbah (August 16, 1895 - March 31, 1935) was born in Nabatieh, Lebanon. He was an electrical and electronics research engineer, mathematician and inventor par excellence. He studied at the American University of Beirut. He taught mathematics at Imperial College of Damascus, Syria, and at the American University of Beirut. He is seen as being the father of the solar cell. He died in an automobile accident at Lewis near Elizabeth Town, New York.

Space Industry (Solar power)

Solar cells have been widely used for space vehicles and satellites as the main source of power. The original solar cell was invented and tested by Mr. Assabbah in 1930; solar power is by far the cleanest and safest source of energy. The solar cell was further developed after World War II by Bell Telephone Laboratories in 1955.

Automotive Industry (The Solar Electric Car)

There are five basic ideas (1929-35) on electric circuits. In 1930, Assabbah performed experiments on his own car to electrify it. He worked seriously to make the idea of the electric car a useful and practical possibility. His early experiments gave GE the unique position as a pioneer in developing the solar cell and sodium-sulphur battery as well. With increasing shortage of liquid fuel, battery-powered electric cars will become attractive for personal transport in and around towns.

Television and Cathode Ray Tube Application

General Electric Company's (GE) research engineers at Schenectady N.Y. developed the Liquid Crystal Display (LCD) instrument system based on the original ideas of Hasan Kamel. It is the world's largest high resolution LCD panel for aircraft. It presents information in colour, and with twice the sharpness of a home TV screen picture.

What do these words and phrases from the text mean? Choose from the following list.

pleasing to the senses, a clear picture, better than anyone else / no one as good as this person, a non-metallic element with symbol S, a picture with detailed image, a machine in orbit around the Earth, something between a solid crystal and a liquid crystal, change the power source into electricity generated, a chemical element with the symbol Na, a device that converts sunlight into electricity, a closed path in which electrons move to produce electric currents

1.) electrify _____

2.) satellite _____

3.) attractive _____

4.) solar cell _____

5.) sulphur _____

6.) sodium _____

7.) electric circuit _____

8.) liquid crystal _____

9.) high resolution _____

10.) sharp picture _____

11.) par excellence _____

Answer these questions in complete sentences.

1.) Who was Hassan Kamel Assabbah?

_____

_____

2.) What is the date of his birth?

_____

_____

3.) What is the date of his death?

_____

_____

4.) Where did he teach Mathematics?

_____

_____

5.) What is he seen as the father of?

_____

_____

6.) In which year did Mr. Assabbah test the first solar cell?

_____

_____

7.) How many basic ideas are there on electric circuits?

_____

_____

8.) Why will battery-powered electric cars become attractive for personal transport in and around towns?

_____

_____

9.) What does LCD stand for?

_____

_____

10.) How does it present information?

_____

_____

Choose *a*, *b*, *c* or *d*.

1.) Hassan Kamel Assabbah died _____

a.) in an LCD   b.) in a car crash   c.) a satellite
d.) in a solar cell

2.) He _____ at the American University of Beirut.

a.) Studyed   b.) studyied   c.) studying   d.) studied

3.) Solar power is the _____ source of energy.

a.) cleanest   b.) cleaner   c.) cleaning   d.) cleaners

4.) The solar cell was further developed _____ Bell Telephone Laboratories.

a.) on   b.) by   c.) buy   d.) after

5.) GE means _____

a.) General Electricity   b.) General Engineers
c.) General Electric   d.) General Engineer

Say if these sentences are true (T) or false (F)

1.) Hassan Kamel Assabbah was a Lebanese national. _____

2.) Solar power is the most dangerous source of energy. _____

3.) Solar cells have never been used for space vehicles. _____

4.) Hassan Kamel electrified another person's car. _____

5.) The LCD is a panel for aircraft._____

UNIT 5
Alexander Graham Bell

Alexander Graham Bell was born in Edinburgh, Scotland, on March 3, 1847.He was a Scottish scientist and inventor best known for inventing the first working telephone in 1876 and founding the Bell Telephone Company in 1877.

Bell's success came through his experiments in sound and the furthering of his family's interest in assisting the deaf with communication. Bell worked with Thomas Watson on the telephone, though his prodigious intellect would allow him to work on numerous other inventions, including flying machines and hydrofoils.

On March 10, 1876, after years of work, Bell perfected his most well-known invention, the telephone, and made his first telephone call. With this success, Bell began to promote the telephone in a series of public demonstrations. At the 1876 Centennial Exhibition in Philadelphia, Bell demonstrated the telephone to the Emperor of Brazil, Dom Pedro, who exclaimed, "Wow, it talks!" Other demonstrations followed, each at a greater distance than the last.

The Bell Telephone Company was organized on July 9, 1877. In January 1915, Bell was invited to make the first transcontinental phone call. From New York, he spoke with his former associate Watson in San Francisco.

What do these words and phrases from the text mean? Choose from the following list.

many,   an inability to hear,   previous,   one hundred years, a public display of items,   a lifting surface or foil that operates in water,   a person's mental power,   a colleague / a co-worker, remarkable in extent / size / degree,   across a continent

1.) deaf _____

2.) prodigious _____

3.) intellect _____

4.) numerous _____

5.) hydrofoil _____

6.) centennial _____

7.) exhibition _____

8.) transcontinental _____

9.) former _____

10.) associate _____

Answer these questions in complete sentences.

1.) Where was Alexander Graham Bell born?

_____

_____

2.) What is he best known for?

_____

_____

3.) What did he found in 1877?

_____

_____

4.) How did Bell's success come?

_____

_____

5.) With whom did Bell work on the telephone?

_____

_____

6.) In which year did Bell perfect the telephone?

_____

_____

7.) How did Bell promote the telephone?

_____

_____

8.) Where was the Centennial Exhibition?

_____

_____

9.) To whom did Bell demonstrate the telephone in 1876?

_____

_____

10.) When did Bell make the first transcontinental phone call?

_____

_____

Choose *a, b, c* or *d*.

1.) Alexander Graham Bell came from _____.

a.) Scotland   b.) England   c.) America   d.) Canada

2.) He _____the Bell Telephone Company in 1877.

a.) found   b.) founding   c.) founded   d.) founds

3.) Bell _____ with Thomas Watson.

a.) worked   b.) work   c.) working   d.) worker

4.) Bell began _____ the telephone in public demonstrations

a.) promote   b.) to promote   c.) promotes   d.) promoter

5.) Bell _____to Watson from New York.

a.) speak   b.) speaking   c.) to speak   d.) spoke

Say if these sentences are true (T) or false (F)

1.) Bell was a scientist and an inventor. _____

2.) His most well-known invention was the phonograph. _____

3.) Dom Pedro was the president of Brazil. _____

4.) The Bell Telephone Company was organised before 1878.

_____

5.) In 1915, Bell made a telephone call from San Francisco to New York. _____

READING FOR PLEASURE
Josiah Wedgewood

The most influential potter in the history of pottery, couldn't use a potter's wheel. But that did not prevent him from building a huge ceramics business. Josiah Wedgwood (1730 – 1795) was a man who triumphed against all odds. After overcoming smallpox in his youth, he later chose to have his right leg amputated to relieve his pain. Although he was left unable to use his beloved potter's wheel, he remained unstoppable in his business. Josiah was a survivor, and his reduced mobility only inspired him to evolve new ways to pursue his objectives.

Wedgwood sought perfection

Thorough, dedicated and determined, Josiah Wedgwood took a very scientific approach to the art of ceramics manufacture. He set himself the ambition of reliably producing a perfect glazed white body and applied himself tirelessly to achieving it. He succeeded in 1761, after 411 experiments. This conviction and professional dedication to manufacturing technique led to changes in production methods which both influenced and helped to shape the Industrial Revolution.

Wedgwood is the first lady's choice

For over two hundred years Wedgwood has been present in the world's most elegant homes. Over the centuries, numerous stately households have had an affinity with Wedgwood. From the holiday palace of Empress Catherine The Great, to the banqueting tables at Queen Elizabeth II's coronation in 1953, via a 1,282 piece dinner service at The White House during President Roosevelt's time in office. Knowing that our tableware continues to be sought-after amongst today's most influential tastemakers is something that brings us inspiration every day.

Answer the questions in complete sentences.

1.) When was Josiah Wedgwood born?

_____

_____

2.) What couldn't he use?

_____

_____

3.) What illness did he have?

_____

_____

4.) Why was his leg amputated?

_____

_____

5.) What did Wedgwood take a scientific approach to?

_____

_____

6.) In which year did he produce a glazed white body?

_____

_____

7.) How many experiments did he do until he successfully produced the glazed white body?

_____

_____

8.) In which year was Queen Elizabeth's coronation?

_____

_____

9.) Who had a holiday palace?

_____

_____

10.) Which US president had a 1,282 piece dinner service in the White House?

_____

_____

THEME 15

GREAT WRITERS

UNIT 1
Charles Dickens

Charles Dickens was born in Portsmouth on 7 February 1812, to John and Elizabeth Dickens. His advantage of being sent to school at the age of nine was short because his father was imprisoned for bad debt. Charles was sent to work in a blacking factory and endured appalling conditions as well as loneliness and despair. After three years he was returned to school, but the experience was never forgotten; it became fictionalised in two of his better-known novels 'David Copperfield' and 'Great Expectations'.

Like many others, he began his literary career as a journalist. His own father became a reporter and Charles began with the journals 'The Mirror of Parliament' and 'The True Sun'. Then in 1833 he became parliamentary journalist for The Morning Chronicle. With new contacts in the press he was able to publish a series of sketches under the pseudonym 'Boz'. In April 1836, he married Catherine Hogarth, daughter of George Hogarth who edited 'Sketches by Boz'. Within the same month came the publication of the extremely successful 'Pickwick Papers', and from that point on there was no looking back for Dickens.

As well as a huge list of novels he published autobiography, edited weekly periodicals including 'Household Words' and 'All Year Round', wrote travel books and administered charitable organisations. He was also a theatre enthusiast, wrote plays and performed before Queen Victoria in 1851. His energy was inexhaustible and he spent much time abroad - for example lecturing against slavery in the United States and touring Italy with companions Augustus Egg and Wilkie Collins, a contemporary writer who inspired Dickens' final unfinished novel 'The Mystery of Edwin Drood'.

What do these words and phrases from the text mean? Choose from the following list.

Writing under a false name / not your real name, a magazine or newspaper published at regular intervals. suffer something patiently, a book written by someone about his/her own life, a person who writes for newspapers / magazines etc, money that one person owes to another, newspapers in general, a long talk on a subject, a person who reports, especially one employed to report news or conduct interviews for the press or broadcasting media, terrible / awful, a paste for cleaning shoes / shoe polish, an organisation which helps the poor, a system which allows fellow human beings to be owned and worked by other human beings, made into a fiction / a story, prepare (written material) for publication by correcting, condensing, or otherwise modifying it. a brief written account of something, someone who is very interested in something, living or happening at the same time, without end, loss of all hope, manage something] / run something, a governing legislature, a close friend, factual written accounts of historical events in their order of time, having no friends or anyone to talk to, a career in writing and publishing

1.) debt _____

2.) blacking _____

3.) endure _____

4.) appalling _____

5.) loneliness _____

6.) despair _____

7.) fictionalised _____

8.) literary career _____

9.) journalist _____

10.) reporter _____

11.) parliament _____

12.) chronicles _____

13.) the press _____

14.) sketch _____

15.) pseudonym _____

16.) inexhaustible _____

17.) administer _____

18.) charitable organisation _____

19.) enthusiast _____

20.) lecture _____

21.) slavery _____

22.) companion _____

23.) contemporary _____

24.) autobiography _____

25.) edit _____

26.) periodical _____

Answer these questions in complete sentences.

1.) Where was Charles Dickens born?

_____

_____

2.) When was he born?

_____

_____

3.) Who were his parents?

_____

_____

4.) How old was Charles Dickens when he was sent to school?

_____

_____

5.) What did Dickens endure in the factory?

_____

_____

6.) How did he begin his literary career?

_____

_____

7.) Which newspaper did he work for in 1833?

_____

_____

8.) Whom did he perform before in 1851?

_____

_____

9.) What did Dickens lecture against?

_____

_____

10.) What was the title of Dicken's unfinished novel?

_____

_____

Choose *a, b, c* or *d*.

1.) Charles Dickens' father was _____ for debt?

a.) prisoned   b.) imprisoned   c.) prison   d.) prisoner

2.) Young Charles Dickens _____ to work in a factory.

a.) was sent   b.) are sent   c.) were sent   d.) was send

3.) Dickens _____ Catherine Hogarth?

a.) marry   b.) marrying   c.) to marry   d.) married

4.) Dickens worked in a _____ factory.

a.) black   b.) blacked   c.) blacks   d.) blacking

5.) Dickens _____ weekly periodicals.

a.) edit   b.) editor   c.) edited   d.) editing

Say if these sentences are true (T) or false (F)

1.) Conditions in the blacking factory were good. _____

2.) Dickens' father became a reporter. _____

3.) 'David Copperfield' was one of Dickens' novels. _____

4.) Dickens got married in August 1836. _____

5.) Dickens didn't like the theatre. _____

UNIT 2
Sir Walter Scott

Sir Walter Scott lived from 15 August 1771 to 21 September 1832. He was the first international novelist. As a poet and as a historical novelist, he was popular throughout the world in his day and people still read his books today. He also did much to create the image that many have today of Scotland, and was among the first to popularise parts of it:

Walter Scott was born in Edinburgh, Scotland, in 1771. His father Walter Scott was a solicitor and his mother Anne was the daughter of a professor of medicine. While a child, Scott contracted polio. He was sent to recuperate with his grandparents in the Scottish Borders for a number of years, where he started to acquire his broad knowledge of Scottish folklore, ballad and legend.

Scott completed his education at Edinburgh High School and Edinburgh University, and went on to practice law. His interest in writing began with two works translated from German, published in 1796.

In 1802-03 Scott's first really important work, *Minstrelsy Of The Scottish Border* appeared. As a became famous with the publication of *The Lay Of The Last Minstrel* (1805) about an old legend from the Borders. It was followed by *Marmion* (1808), a historical romance. The *Lady In The Lake* appeared in 1810 and *Rokeby* in 1813. The last of Scott's major poems, *Lord Of The Isles*, was published in 1815. In 1806 he started a printing and publishing business with his friend James Ballantyne.

He produced a series of Scottish novels in quick succession, culminating with *Rob Roy*, published in 1817, which sold its original print run of 10,000 in two weeks.

Ivanhoe, published in 1819, was set in the England of King Richard I, and its success started a second series of novels, again produced in rapid order.

Scott's company Ballantyne's collapsed in 1825, leaving him with considerable debts. He worked with renewed determination to write his way out of his problems and placed his home, Abbotsford, and his income into a special fund belonging to his creditors. Scott died at Abbotsford in 1832 and was buried in the ruins of Dryburgh Abbey. He hadn't cleared his debts by the time of his death, but his posthumous earnings ensured that his creditors were all eventually paid in full.

What do these words and phrases from the text mean? Choose from the following list.

a type of monastery used by a religious order, a mental picture, the books printed in a single printing job, something that happens after the death of the person who started something, make something new, a traditional story sometimes popularly regarded as historical but not authenticated, recover / get well, a book with a story about love, a strong and enthusiastic wish to do something, everything paid, a person or company to whom money is owed, to get / obtain, the traditional beliefs, customs, and stories of a community passed through the generations by word of mouth, a person who writes novels, a poem or song telling a story in short verses, traditional stories in song and dance, a lawyer, one thing following another very quickly, a disease that cripples, pay off creditors and finish the debts, someone who writes poetry, to make sure of / be certain, to reach a point of highest development, someone

who writes novels based on an era in history,   get an illness,
make something popular,   an amount of money – usually
deposited in a bank account,   when a company goes bankrupt

1.) novelist _____

2.) poet _____

3.) historical novelist _____

4.) image _____

5.) popularise _____

6.) solicitor _____

7.) contract an illness _____

8.) polio _____

9.) recuperate _____

10.) folklore _____

11.) ballad _____

12.) legend _____

13.) minstrelsy _____

14.) romance _____

15.) quick succession _____

16.) culminate _____

17.) print run _____

18.) company collapse _____

19.) renewed _____

20.) determination _____

21.) fund _____

22.) creditor _____

23.) abbey _____

24.) clear debts _____

25.) posthumous _____

26.) paid in full _____

27.) acquire _____

28.) ensure _____

Answer these questions in complete sentences.

1.) What did Sir Walter Scott create about Scotland?

_____

_____

2.) In which country was Scott born?

_____

_____

3.) In which city was he born?

_____

_____

4.) Which disease did Scott contract when he was a child?

_____

_____

5.) With whom did he recuperate?

_____

_____

6.) Where did he acquire his broad knowledge of Scottish folklore, ballad, and legend?

_____

_____

7.) Where did Scott complete his education?

_____

_____

8.) What was the name of Scott's first really important work?

_____

_____

9.) When did Scott's company collapse?

_____

_____

10.) Where was Scott buried?

_____

_____

Choose *a, b, c* or *d*.

1.) Scott was the first _____ novelist.

a.) national   b.) nation   c.) international   d.) nations

2.) Scott _____ in 1771.

a.) was born   b.) is born   c.) were born   d.) are borned

3.) Scott _____ to practice law.

a.) went in   b.) go on   c.) went on   d.) on

4.) Scott had _____ debts.

a.) consider   b.) considering   c.) considers   d.) considerable

5.) He produced a series of _____ novels.

a.) Scotland   b.) Scottish   c.) Scot   d.) Scotty

Say if these sentences are true (T) or false (F)

1.) Scott lived until August 15th 1771. _____

2.) He and James Ballantyne started a printing and publishing business. _____

3.) *Ivanhoe* was set in the England of King Richard II. _____

4.) The name of his home was Abbotsford. _____

5.) Scott had paid off all his debts by the time he died. _____

UNIT 3
Khahil Gibran

Kahlil Gibran, was born January 6, 1883, in Bsharri, Lebanon. He was the youngest son of Khalil Sa'd Jubran, a tax collector and Kamila Jubran. In 1885 Gibran emigrated with his mother and siblings to the United States.

At the age of 15, Gibran was sent by his mother to Beirut, Lebanon, to attend school. He returned to Boston in 1902. In that year and the one that followed, Gibran's sister, Sultana, brother Bhutros, and mother died. His remaining sister Marianna supported herself and Gibran from her earnings as a dressmaker.

In 1904 Gibran began publishing articles in an Arabic-language newspaper and also had his first public exhibit of his drawings, which were praised by the Boston photographer Fred Holland Day. Mary Haskell, who ran an all-girls school became Gibran's lifelong patron, paying for him to study art at the Académie Julian in Paris in 1908.

Haskell also enabled Gibran's move to New York City in 1911. At a lunch in the New York, Gibran met Alfred Knopf, who became his publisher. In 1918, Gibran's book of poems called *The Madman* was published.

Gibran was active in a New York-based Arab-American literary group called the Pen League, whose members promoted writing in Arabic and English. Throughout his life he published nine books in Arabic and eight in English, which ruminate on love, longing, and death.

He died of cirrhosis of the liver on April 10, 1931, in New York City.

What do these words and phrases from the text mean? Choose from the following list.

a picture in black and white drawn with a pencil,   think very deeply about something,   someone who collects tax money for the government,   to say very good things about someone or something,   a brother or a sister,   a deadly disease which affects the liver,   the money you get from salary or business, support something and further its progress,   to leave your country and go and live in another one,   an exhibition where the public can see the things on display,   a group of people interested in literature,   someone (usually a woman) who makes dresses,   a person who gives financial or other support to a person or organisation

1.) tax collector _____

2.) emigrate _____

3.) sibling _____

4.) earnings _____

5.) dressmaker _____

6.) public exhibit _____

7.) drawing _____

8.) praise _____

9.) patron _____

10.) literary group _____

11.) promote _____

12.) ruminate _____

13.) cirrhosis of the liver _____

Answer these questions in complete sentences.

1.) Where was Kahil Gibran born?

_____

_____

2.) What was his nationality?

_____

_____

3.) Was he the eldest or the youngest in the family?

_____

_____

4.) What was his father"s job?

_____

_____

5.) Where did Gibran and his family emigrate to?

_____

_____

6.) How did his remaining sister support them?

_____

_____

7.) What was the language od the newspaper that Gibran started publishing articles in?

_____

_____

8.) Who praised Gebran's drawings?

_____

_____

9.) Who became Gibran's lifelong patron?

_____

_____

10.) What was the New York based Arab – American literary group called?

_____

_____

Choose *a*, *b*, *c*, or d

1. Gabran was born in _____

   a.) Syria b.___) Lebanon   c.) Sudan d .) The US

2. In _____ Gibran emigrated to the US

   a.) 8185   b.) 8581   c.) 8518 d) 1885

3. He returned to _____in 1902.

   a.) Boston b,) New York   c.) Chicago d,) Harlem

4. Haskel also _____Gibran's return to New York City.

   a.) enables   b.) enabling   c) enable   d) enabled

5. He _____ of cirrhosis of the liver.

   a.) die   b.) dying c,) died   d.) die

Say if these sentences are True (T) or False (F)

1. Gabran was born in the 19th century _____

2. Gabran was sent to school in Beirut _____

3. Gabran was a great scientist _____

4. Gabran exhibited is paintings_____

5. He died in 1932.-_____

FRANCIS A. ANDREW

UNIT 4
James Fennimore Cooper

James Fennimore Cooper (1789-1851) was a prolific American writer who spent most of his life in Cooperstown, New York, near a lake surrounded by the Iroquois Indians. Cooper crafted a unique form of literature writing about frontier and Indian life. He wrote historical novels known as *The Leatherstocking Tales*. His masterpiece considered *The Last of the Mohicans* (1826), set in 1757 during the French and Indian War. It gained Cooper fame and notoriety, and remains a standard in most American literature courses. Themes contrasting wilderness versus civilization, were common to many of his novels and stories.

Cooper's novel *The Pioneers* (1823), and his short story *The Lake Gun*, set at Lake Seneca, are well known. Cooper spent seven years in Europe at the height of his popularity, before returning to the U.S., where he became obsessed with writing naval histories and seafaring stories into his later years.

Cooper died in 1851, and is considered one of the most popular 19th century authors, influencing the type of Henry David Thoreau's writing, yet he remained more popular in Europe than at home. Honore de Balzac and Leo Tolstoy admired Cooper's work. One of Cooper's legacies was he was one of the first American authors to incorporate African, African-American, and native Indian characters in his stories.

What do the following words and phrases mean/? Choose from the following list.

of note / of ill fame,   a great writer / one who writes a lot,   a great work,   college degree courses on literature,   maker, having a strong will,   connected with the navy and the sea, regular / normal,   journeys on the sea,   on the edge of the known territory

234

1.) prolific writer _____

_____

2.) crafter _____

_____

3.) frontier_____

_____

4.) masterpiece_____

_____

5.) notoriety_____

_____

6.) standard_____

_____

7.) literature course_____

_____

8.) obsessed_____

_____

9.) naval_____

_____

10.)seafaring _____

_____

Answer the following questions in complete sentences.

1.) When was James Fennimore Cooper born?

_____

_____

2.) Where did he spend most of his life?

_____

_____

3.) Which tribe of Indians lived near the lake?

_____

_____

4.) What was the name of his masterpiece ?

_____

_____

5.) What did it gain for Cooper?

_____

_____

6.) What were common in the themes of many of his novels?

_____

_____

7.) Where was his novel *The lake Gun set*?

_____

_____

8.) How long did Cooper stay in Europe?

_____

_____

9.) What did he become obsessed with writing?

_____

_____

10.) Who admired Cooper's work?

_____

_____

Choose *a*, *b*, *c*, or *d*

1.) Cooper was _____ writer

   a a British   b an Indian   c. an American   d a Russian

2.) Cooper_____ stories about Indian and frontier life.

   a. craft   b crafted   c crafting   d has crafted

3.) *The Last of the Mohicans* _____ a standard in most American literary courses.

   a. remain   b. remaining   c. remains   d. to remain

4.) The pioneers was written_____ 1823.

   a. on   b since   c. to d. in

5.) Cooper was _____ in Europe than at home.

   a. more popular   b. most popular   c. the popular
   d. the most popular

Say if these sentences are right or wrong.

1.) *The Leatherstocking Tales* are seafaring stories.-_____

2.) The French fought against the Indians._____

3.) *The Lake Gun* was a long story. _____

4.) It was set at Lake Iroquois._____

5.) Cooper is considered one of the least popular authors of the 19th century_____

UNIT 5
Robert Louis Stevenson

Born on November 13, 1850, in Edinburgh, Scotland, Robert Louis Balfour Stevenson came from a family of prominent lighthouse engineers. During his boyhood, he spent holidays with his maternal grandfather. Prone to illness, Stevenson spent many of his early winters in bed, entertained only by his imagination and a great love of reading, especially <u>William Shakespeare</u>, Sir Walter Scott, John Bunyan, and *The Arabian Nights*.

Encouraged to follow the family tradition of lighthouse engineering, he began studies at the University of Edinburgh in 1867, but quickly discovered he preferred a career in literature. To satisfy his father, he acquired a law degree and was admitted made a lawyer by the time he was twenty-five.

Stevenson spent the next four years traveling through Europe, mostly around Paris, publishing essays and articles about his travels. In 1876, he met Fanny Vandegrift Osbourne, a married woman ten years his elder. When she decided to return to San Francisco soon after they met, Stevenson followed, taking the long voyage across the Atlantic and across the United States against the advice of his friends and physician. To add to his adventure, he chose to travel in steerage and was near death when he arrived in Monterey, California, in 1879. After being nursed back to health, he continued to San Francisco that winter, though it cost him his health. Osbourne, who had since been divorced, helped him recover. They married the following May.

After several months in the U.S. with his wife and her young son, Stevenson brought his family back to Britain. Frequently sick, he continued to write seriously, producing the bulk of his best-loved work. His first successful novel, *Treasure Island* was published in 1884, followed by *A Child's Garden of Verses* in 1885, and *The Strange Case of Dr. Jekyll and Mr. Hyde* in 1886.

Following the death of his father in 1887, Stevenson left again for the U.S. with his family, planning a move to Colorado. He died in1894.

What do the following words and phrases mean Choose from the following list.

part of a ship providing the cheapest form of transport, a structure with a beacon of light to guide or warn ships at sea, likely or liable to suffer from something, the marriage is finished, important, the most part, a medical doctor, your mother's father

1.) prominent _____

_____

2.) lighthouse_____

_____

3.) maternal grandfather_____

_____

4.) prone_____

_____

5.) physician_____

_____

6.) steerage_____

_____

7.) divorced_____

_____

8.) bulk_____

_____

Answer the questions in complete sentences.

1.) What year was Robert Louis Stevenson born in? _____

_____

2.) What kind of engineers were his family?_____

_____

3.) Whom did he spend holidays with?_____

_____

4.) What authors did he read?_____

_____

5.) What did he do to satisfy his father?_____

_____

6.) Where did Stevenson mostly travel?_____

_____

7.) Whom did he meet in 1876?_____

_____

8.) What was his first successful novel?_____

_____

9.) When was The Strange Case of Dr Jekyll and Mr Hyde published?_____

_____

10.) When did return to the US?_____

_____

Choose *a, b, c,* or *d*

1.) Robert Louis Stevenson _____ born in Edinburgh

   a. is   b. were   c. are   d. was

2.) Stevenson _____ many of his winters in bed.

   a. spent   b. spending   c. spend   d. spender

3.) A Child's Garden of Verses was published in _____

   a. 1885   b. 8218   c. 8518   d 1858

4.) Stevenson _____ his family back to Britain.

   a. bring   b. bringing   c. brought   d. to bringing

5.) He continued _____ seriously

   a. write   b. writes   c wrote   d. to write

Say if these sentences are true or false

1.) Stevenson was never prone to illness_____

2.) He began studies at the University of Aberdeen_____

3.) He studied law_____

4.) He had a preference for literature_____

5.) He met Fanny Vandegrift Osbourne in 1877_____

READING FOR ENJOYMENT
COCOA

Cocoa is the key ingredient in chocolate and chocolate confections.

The cocoa bean is the seed of the cacao tree (*Theobroma cacao*), a tropical plant which is found to the equatorial regions of the Americas. From the processed cocoa bean comes the fluid paste, or liquor, from which cocoa powder and chocolate are made. Chocolate is sold directly to the consumer as solid bars of eating chocolate, as packaged cocoa, and as baking chocolate.

Christopher Columbus took cocoa beans to Spain after his fourth voyage in 1502, and the Spanish conquistadores, arriving in Mexico in 1519, were introduced to a chocolate beverage by the Aztec. The Aztec beverage was made from sun-dried shelled beans, probably fermented in their pods. The broken kernels, or nibs, were roasted in earthen pots and then ground to a paste in a concave stone, called a *metate*, over a small fire. Vanilla and various spices and herbs were added, and corn (maize) was sometimes used to produce milder flavour.

Too bitter for European taste, the mixture was sweetened with sugar when introduced to Spain. Although Spain guarded the secret of its *xocoatl* beverage for almost 100 years, it reached Italy in 1606 and became popular in France. By 1765 chocolate manufacture had begun in the <u>American colonies</u> at Dorchester, in <u>Massachusetts,</u> using cocoa beans from the <u>West Indies</u>.

Answer the questions in complete sentences

1.) Where is the theobrama cocoa plant found?

_____

_____

2.) What comes from the process the bean?

_____

_____

3.) How is cocoa sold directly to the consumer?

_____

_____

4.) Who took the bean to Spain?

_____

_____

5.) What was the Aztec beverage made from?

_____

_____

6.) Where were the broken kernels or nibs roasted?

_____

_____

7.) How did the Spanish deal with the bitter taste?

_____

_____

8.) How long did Spain guard the secret of xocoatl?

_____

_____

9.) When did it reach Italy?

_____

_____

10.) When did the manufacture of chocolate begin/?

_____

_____

THEME 16

THE BICYCLE

UNIT 1
The invention of the bicycle

Historians disagree about the invention of the bicycle, and many dates have been suggested. It is most likely that no individual is the inventor and that the bicycle evolved through the efforts of many. Although Leonardo da Vinci was thought to have sketched a bicycle in 1492,the drawing was discovered to be a forgery added in the 1960s.

The first two-wheeled rider-propelled machine for which there is indisputable evidence was the *draisienne*, invented by Baron Karl von Drais de Sauerbrun of Germany. In 1817 he rode it for 14 km (9 miles), and the following year he exhibited it in Paris. Although von Drais called his device a *Laufmaschine* ("running machine"), *draisienne* and *velocipede* became more popular names. The machine was made of wood, and the seated rider propelled himself by paddling his feet against the ground. A balance board supported the rider's arms. Although von Drais was granted patents, copies were soon being produced in other countries, including Great Britain, Austria, Italy, and the United States.

Denis Johnson of London purchased a *draisienne* and patented an improved model in 1818. The following year he produced more than 300, and they became commonly known as hobby-horses. They were very expensive, and many buyers were members of the nobility. Caricaturists called the devices "dandy horses," and riders were sometimes jeered in public. The design raised health concerns, and riding proved impractical except on smooth roads. Johnson's production ended after only six months. The brief *draisienne*–hobby-horse fad did not lead to sustained development

245

of two-wheeled vehicles, but von Drais and Johnson established that the machines could remain balanced while in motion. For the next 40 years, most experimenters focused on human-powered three- and four-wheeled machines.

There is evidence that a small number of two-wheeled machines with rear treadle drives were built in southwestern Scotland during the early 1840s. Kirkpatrick Macmillan, a blacksmith of Dumfriesshire, is most often associated with these. He is said to have traveled 40 miles (64 km) to Glasgow in 1842, although documentation is problematic. Gavin Dalzell of Lesmahagow probably built a similar two-wheeled machine in the mid-1840s and is said to have operated it for many years. This may be the heavily restored machine in the Glasgow Museum of Transport. It has wooden wheels and iron rims. The rider's feet swung treadles back and forth, moving a pair of rods connected to cranks on the rear wheels. Thomas McCall, another Scotsman, built similar machines in the late 1860s. Documents indicate that Alexandre Lefèbvre of Saint-Denis, France, built a two-wheeled velocipede powered by treadles connected to cranks on the rear wheel in 1842. Lefèbvre took his velocipede with him when he immigrated to California in 1861, and it still exists there in the History San José museum. Neither the Scottish nor Lefèbvre's machines were commercially exploited, and there is no evidence that they contributed to subsequent development.

The word *bicycle* came into use in Europe in 1868 to replace the cumbersome *vélocipède de pedale*. The first velocipede powered via pedals mounted on the front wheel was built in Paris during the early 1860s.

What do the following words and phrases mean Choose from the following list.

of a problem / creating a problem,   pushing with your feet,   the back,   something that is worked with your feet, something that cannot be challenged / the evidence for it is great,

1.) rider-propelled

2.) indisputable

3.) padding your feet

4.) nobility

5.) impractical

6.) smooth

7.) sustained

8.) treadle

9.) blacksmith

10.) problematic

11.) rod

12.) crank

13.) rear

14.) exploited

15.) subsequent

16.) cumbersome

17.) mounted

18.) pedal

THEME 17

TRADING IN OMAN

UNIT 1
Trade in the past

Revision: The present simple tense in the active voice.

Ali gets up every morning at 6 o'clock. He has a shower and then goes to the kitchen. His mother prepares breakfast for him and his siblings. A bus then takes Ali to school. When he is in class, he opens the books on his desk. He gives the teacher his homework. He eats his dinner at midday. At the end of the day, the bus takes Ali and his siblings back home. "We clean the house before dinner," says Ali. "My father sometimes gives me money to buy sweets."

The present simple tense in the passive voice. The words in *italics* are where the above paragraph has been changed into the passive voice.

Ali gets up every morning at 6 o'clock. He has a shower and then goes to the kitchen. *Breakfast is prepared for Ali and his siblings by his mother. Ali is taken to school by a bus.* When he is in class, *the books on his desk are opened by him. His homework is given to the teacher by him. Dinner is eaten by him at midday.* At the end of the day, *Ali and his siblings are taken back home by the bus.* "*The house is cleaned by us before dinner,*" says Ali. "*Money is sometimes given to me by my father to buy sweets.*"

Change the following paragraph into the present simple passive voice

Ahmed is an engineer. He builds bridges. He drives his car to work every day. He checks the machines in the factory. He speaks to the workers. He tells them about the work plans. Ahmed then looks

248

at the new bridge. Ahmed explains some things to the foreman. The foreman listens to Ahmed. He writes down some things in his notebook. Ahmed buys his lunch from a restaurant near his office.

_____

_____

_____

_____

_____

_____

_____

_____

_____

Read

Frankincense was traditionally harvested by making a shallow cut into the bark of the *Boswellia sacra* tree. The sap of the tree oozed out and began to harden into a resinous substance. This was then collected. It was stored in caves to dry out. Once dry, it was sent to Khor Rorī and Al-Bilad for export to India or to Egypt and Palestine. It was taken to these places by camel in a caravan that traversed the overland trail.

There is something about Dhofar which results in the production of this top-quality frankincense? 'A note on the Dhofar province, southern Arabia' was prepared in 1943 by a British official called G. N. Jackson. The quality of the frankincense resin was affected by the geography of Dhofar and the distribution of moisture there.

What do these words and phrases from the paragraphs mean? Choose from the following list.

someone who has authority – usually from a government,   a brother or sister,   someone in charge of a squad of workers, wetness,   a crop,   to flow slowly out of something,   not deep,   12 o'clock noon,   influence,   the outer part of a tree trunk,   a route that goes on land,   physical material, bring together into one place,   to move over / along / through, chocolates / candy / sugary substances,   a notepad for quickly writing things in,   the fluid part of a plant

1.) midday _____

2.) sibling _____

3.) sweets _____

4.) foreman _____

5.) notebook _____

6.) harvest _____

7.) shallow _____

8.) bark _____

9.) sap _____

10.) ooze _____

11.) resin _____

12.) substance _____

13.) collect _____

14.) traverse _____

15.) overland trail _____

16.) an official _____

17.) affect _____

18.) moisture _____

Answer the questions using the passive voice in the past simple

1.) How was frankincense traditionally harvested?

_____

_____

2.) What happened to the sap after it oozed out and began to harden into a resinous substance?

_____

_____

3.) What happened next?

_____

_____

4.) What happened when it was dry?

_____

_____

5.) How was it exported?

_____

_____

6.) When was the note on the Dhofar province prepared?

_____

_____

7.) Who was the note prepared by?

_____

_____

8.) What was the quality of the frankincense resin affected by?

_____

_____

Revision: The present continuous tense active voice

Salwa and Muneera are in the supermarket. They are buying some food. Salwa and Muneera are pushing trolleys up and down the aisles. Salwa is looking at some tins of soup. Muneera is checking the prices of chicken. Now they are taking their purchases to the checkout. The lady at the checkout is checking out their items.

The present continuous tense in the passive voice. The words in *italics* are where the above paragraph has been changed into the passive voice.

The present continuous tense passive voice

Salwa and Muneera are in the supermarket. *Some food is being bought by them. Trolleys are being pushed up and down the aisles by them. Some tins of soup are being looked at by Salwa. The prices of chicken are being checked by Muneera. Their purchases are being taken to the checkout by them. Their items are being checked out by the lady at the checkout.*

Change the following into the present continuous passive

Yousef and Sameer are in a street. They are looking at the street. They can see cars, buses and lorries. A policeman is directing traffic. A man is parking his car. Some men are building a house. A shopkeeper is cleaning a shop window. A waiter is bringing some tea and cakes to some people. Two boys are flying kites in the park.

_____

_____

_____

_____

_____

_____

_____

_____

_____

_____

_____

What do these words and phrases from the paragraphs mean? Choose from the following list.

things,   a passageway separating shelves in a supermarket, the part of the supermarket where you pay for your good,   a cart with wheels for keeping your goods in,   things you buy,   a light frame covered with paper,   cloth,   or plastic,   often provided with a stabilizing tail,   and designed to be flown in the air at the end of a long string,   a cheap metal,   liquid food especially with a meat, fish, or vegetable stock as a base and often containing pieces of solid food, controlling the flow and movement of vehicles on the street, soup contained in tin cans

1.) trolley _____

2.) aisle _____

3.) tin _____

4.) soup _____

5.) purchases _____

6.) items _____

7.) checkout _____

8.) directing traffic _____

9.) kite _____

10.) tins of soup _____

UNIT 2
A visit to the souk

Revision: The present perfect tense

John is in his manager's office. The manager is asking him about the jobs John and his co-workers have completed.

Manager: Have you done the stocktaking John?

John: Yes, I have completed the stocktaking.

Manager: And have you written the report for the directors?

John: No, I haven't done that yet.

Manager: Has the accountant sent the invoice to the customers yet?

John: Yes he has. He has already sent it.

Manager: Has the delivery lorry driver delivered the furniture to Mrs. Thomas?

John: No, he hasn't delivered it yet.

What do these words and phrases from the dialogue mean? Choose from the following list.

making a list of all the goods in a shop or company,   a list of goods with the prices on it,   to bring to someone,   a fellow worker / someone who works with you,   someone who handles the money of a company,   a written account of something, the highest level of authority in a company

1.) co-worker _____

2.) stocktaking _____

3.) report _____

4.) directors _____

5.) accountant _____

6.) invoice _____

7.) deliver _____

Write these sentences using the present perfect tense. Look at the verb in brackets ()

Examples: Bobby _____an email. (send)

Bobby has sent an email.

Barry and Harry _____the car yet. (no / fix)

Barry and Harry haven't fixed the car yet.

1.) Mr. Jakes _____out. (go)

_____

_____

2.) The manager and the supervisor _____to the workers yet. (no / speak)

_____

_____

3.) Ahmed _____a new car. (buy)

_____

_____

4.) My parents _____to Spain. (no / be)

_____

_____

5.) The driver _____yet. (no/ arrive)

_____

_____

6.) The plane _____just _____. (land)

_____

_____

7.) The boys _____already _____their homework. (do)

_____

_____

8.) The cat _____its milk yet. (no / drink)

_____

_____

9.) The chairs and tables _____. (no / deliver)

_____

_____

10.)My friends _____just _____arrived. (come)

_____

_____

Read

Jasim went to the souk yesterday. He is telling his friend Kamal about it.

Kamal: What did you do at the souk yesterday?

Jasim: I had just arrived at the souk when I saw some very interesting things in a shop.

Kamal: What kind of shop was it?

Jasim: It was a shop selling traditional arts and crafts. The shop had just opened when I decided to go in and have a look at it.

Kamal: Did you go in?

Jasim: I had just gone in when the owner offered me some coffee and dates.

Kamal: That was nice of him. What did you do next?

Jasim: When I had finished drinking my coffee and eating the dates, I looked at the artifacts in the shop.

Kamal: What were some of the things the shop had?

Jasim: There were khanjars of many different sizes. Some were made of metal, and some were made of wood. After I had seen the khanjars, I saw some wooden models of traditional Omani boats called dhows. The owner, Mr. Malik, told me he had carved some of them himself.

Kamal: Mr. Malik must be a very talented man. What else did you see after you had seen the khanjars and the dhows?

Jasim: I saw some replicas of old firearms. And I admired the handcrafted dolls and the handcrafted models of Nizwa Fort.

Kamal: Were the artefacts expensive?

Jasim: After I had finished browsing around the displays, I asked Mr. Malik about the prices. Some things were expensive, but some things were quite cheap.

Kamal: Did you buy anything after you had asked about the prices?

Jasim: Yes I did. I bought a small model of Nizwa Fort.

Kamal: That's great. Do you have it here now? Can I see it?

Jasim: Well after I had bought the model, I took it home. After I had taken it home, I gave it to my grandmother as a present.

Kamal: That was nice. I'm sure she liked it.

Jasim: She did. After I had given it to her, she thanked me very much for it.

What do these words and phrases from the text mean? Choose from the following list.

something made of wood,   a person to whom something belongs,   a gun / a weapon,   to shape a piece of wood or metal into a recognisable object,   things made by hand and not by machines, a gift, someone who is very good at doing something, something in miniature representing a larger thing, to look at something in an approving way, something which shows human workmanship, a small miniature of a human being made of wood or plastic, casually looking around a shop or an exhibition, an object which looks exactly like a historical item but is made in the modern period

1.) arts and crafts _____

2.) artifact _____

3.) wooden _____

4.) model _____

5.) owner _____

6.) carve _____

7.) replica _____

8.) talented _____

9.) admire _____

10.) doll _____

11.) firearm _____

12.) browsing _____

13.) present _____

Answer these questions using the past perfect tense

1.) What happened when Jasim arrived at the souk yesterday?

_____

_____

2.) What did Jasim do when the shop had just opened?

_____

_____

3.) What did the owner of the shop do when Jasim had gone in?

_____

_____

4.) What did Jasim do after he had finished drinking his coffee and eating his dates?

_____

_____

5.) What did Jasim see after he had seen the khanjars?

_____

_____

6.) What had Mr. Malik told Jasim?

_____

_____

7.) What did Kamal see after he had seen the khanjars and dhows?

_____

_____

8.) What did Jasim do after he had finished browsing the displays?

_____

_____

9.) What did Jasim do after he had bought the model of Nizwa Fort?

_____

_____

10.) What did Jasim do after he had taken the model home?

_____

_____

11.) What did Jasim's grandmother do after he had given her the model?

_____

_____

Complete these sentences using the past perfect and the past simple. Choose from the verbs in brackets ().

Example: I _____my dinner, when the phone _____. (finish / ring)

I had just finished my dinner when the phone rang.

1.) John _____out of his house when he _____his friend. (go / see)

_____

_____

2.) I _____my car to the supermarket when it _____down. (drive / break)

_____

_____

3.) The cars _____ to the crossroads when the traffic lights _____ to red. (get / change)

_____

_____

4.) After we _____ dinner, we _____ to the football match. (eat / go)

_____

_____

5.) After the team _____ a goal, the fans _____. (score / cheer)

_____

_____

6.) Before mother _____ to the supermarket, she _____ the dinner. (go / cook)

_____

_____

7.) The children _____ their homework before they _____ television. (do / watch)

_____

_____

8.) The manager _____ an email after he _____ a phone call. (send /make)

_____

_____

9.) The pupils _____down at their desks after they _____into the classroom. (sit /come)

_____

_____

10.)The bird _____in the sky before it _____to its nest. (fly /fly)

_____

_____

UNIT 3
A shipwreck

Revision: The past continuous active and the past continuous passive

Ahmed and Sameer were at a football match yesterday. Many things were happening. The players were scoring goals during the match. The referee showed a player a red card. The fans were cheering on the teams. Some of the fans were waving scarves with their teams' colours. The crowd was singing songs. At half time, Ahmed was drinking a bottle of water and Sameer was eating a sandwich. TV cameramen were filming the match.

The present continuous tense in the passive voice. The words in *italics* are where the above paragraph has been changed into the passive voice.

Ahmed and Sameer were at a football match yesterday. Many things were happening. *Some goals were being scored by the players during the match. A player was being shown a red card by the referee. The teams were being cheered on by the fans. Scarves showing the teams' colours were being waved by some of the fans. Songs were being sung by the crowd. At half-time, a bottle of water was being drunk by Ahmed and a sandwich was being eaten by Sameer. The match was being filmed by TV cameramen.*

Answer the following questions using the past continuous passive

1.) What was being scored during the match?

_____

_____

2.) What can you say about the player and the referee?

_____

_____

3.) Who were the teams being cheered on by?

_____

_____

4.) What was being waved?

_____

_____

5.) Who were songs being sung by?

_____

_____

6.) What was being drunk by Ahmed?

_____

_____

7.) What was being eaten by Sameer?

_____

_____

8.) Who was the match being filmed by?

_____

_____

Change the following sentences from the past continuous active into the past continuous passive.

1.) I was baking a cake yesterday.

_____

_____

2.) The teams were playing a match last week.

_____

_____

3.) The mechanics were fixing the engine this morning.

_____

_____

4.) The lorries were delivering the good to the supermarket.

_____

_____

5.) The bus was taking the passengers into town.

_____

_____

6.) The burglar was robbing the house?

_____

_____

7.) You were writing a letter.

_____

_____

8.) My sister was baking some cakes.

_____

_____

Change these passive sentences from the past continuous passive to the past continuous active

1.) Books were being read by us this morning.

_____

_____

2.) Food was being bought by the customers.

_____

_____

3.) A plane was being flown by Captain Muneer.

_____

_____

4.) The floor was being swept by the cleaner.

_____

_____

5.) The horse was being ridden by Ali.

_____

_____

6.) The computer was being rebooted by the IT expert.

_____

_____

7.) Exams were being given by the teachers.

_____

_____

8.) Tea and coffee were being brought by the waiters.

_____

_____

9.) Patients were being treated by the doctors.

_____

_____

10.) Cars were being driven by the drivers.

_____

_____

Read

In 2013, the Oman Ministry of Heritage and Culture and a British company called Blue Water Recoveries found a shipwreck off the coast of Oman.

Five hundred years ago a Portuguese ship, named the Esmeralda, sank during a violent storm off the coast of Oman. The ship and its crew were lost.

In 2013, portions of the wreckage were found off the coast of Oman on Al Hallaniyah Island. Archaeologists from the UK and Oman dived to the seabed where they discovered the remains of the Esmerelda.

While looking through the debris, the divers also came across a very rare silver coin called the Indio. Today, only two of these coins exist in the whole world.

"That was an amazing discovery," said Mr Mearns. "It was like a thing you read about in a Hollywood story."

This was the first underwater excavation carried out in Oman, according to Ayoub al-Baisaidi, who is the supervisor of marine archaeology at the Oman Ministry of Heritage and Culture. "Oman is now looking at outside archives to find out about the relationships and trade between Oman and the outside world."

What do these words and phrases from the text mean? Choose from the following list.

a badly damaged ship now under the sea,   do a task / job, someone who goes under the sea,   digging into the ground to discover things from the past,   how people or countries interact, past of sink / to go down under the sea,   extremely strong wind and rain,   files of documents from the past,   the parts of a ship wreck,   you can see it now,   the people who work on a ship,   people who dig up the past,   connected to the sea,   to go under the sea,   not many of something / very few left,   parts of,   what remains of a large thing which has been destroyed,   round metallic money,   find,   the floor / bottom of the sea

1.) shipwreck _____

2.) violent storm _____

3.) crew _____

4.) sank _____

5.) portions _____

6.) wreckage _____

7.) archaeologists _____

8.) dive _____

9.) seabed _____

10.) debris _____

11.) come across _____

12.) coin _____

13.) rare _____

14.) exist _____

15.) excavation _____

16.) carry out _____

17.) marine _____

18.) archives _____

19.) relationship _____

20.) diver _____

Answer the questions in complete sentences. Use the same verb tenses of the questions in your answers.

1.) Who found a shipwreck off the coast of Oman?

_____

_____

2.) When was it found?

_____

_____

3.) Where was the wreck found?

_____

_____

4.) What was the name of the ship that had sunk?

_____

_____

5.) How long ago had it sunk?

_____

_____

6.) Which country had the ship come from?

_____

_____

7.) What had caused the ship to sink?

_____

_____

8.) Why is the Indio rare?

_____

_____

9.) Who said it was an amazing discovery?

_____

_____

10.) Who is Ayoub Al Baisaidi?

_____

_____

11.) Why are the outside archives being read by Oman?

_____

_____

Say if the <u>underlined</u> verbs in these sentences are present simple active,   present simple passive,   present continuous active, present continuous passive,   present perfect,   past perfect, past simple active,   past simple passive

1.) Tommy and I <u>had done</u> our work when the manager <u>came</u> in.

_____

_____

2.) I <u>am doing</u> my homework now. _____

3.) The dinner <u>is cooked</u>. _____

4.) The books <u>are being put</u> _____

5.) The ship <u>was sunk</u> in a violent storm. _____

6.) My friends and I <u>played</u> football yesterday. _____

7.) The boy <u>opened</u> his birthday present. _____

8.) Tammy <u>goes</u> to work by bus every day. _____

9.) The reports <u>were given</u> to the manager by the secretary.

_____

10.) They <u>have bought</u> a new house. _____

11.) John <u>has got</u> a new job. _____

12.) The mechanics <u>are repairing</u> the car now. _____

13.) The pizzas <u>are being delivered</u> now. _____

14.) The boss <u>read</u> an email after he <u>had switched</u> on the computer.

_____

_____

15.) The lost money <u>was found</u> this morning. _____

16.) He has been to China. He went there last year.

_____

_____

17.) The house was being cleaned yesterday. _____

18.) The chicken was eaten by a fox. _____

19.) John reads a newspaper in the morning._____

20.) I ate my lunch at one o'clock. _____

UNIT 4
Bahla Souq

The traditional souqs of Bahla, with their ancient lanes, ancient masjid and its 13km-long wall that dates back to pre-Islamic times makes it a major tourist attraction.

Bahla souk is a wonder that transports the visitor back in time. Located at the foot of the western slope of the plateau, the souq area covers about 4493 square metres. The souq's actual measurement is 80 metres in length and 65 metres in width.

The souq includes a collection of 142 shops where products vary from food, to household items, to herbs and spices and some traditional items

The souq was originally built with mud bricks but some of its shops were renovated just recently and now are partly made of concrete blocks. Located at the heart of the city's commercial district, the souq has seen many renovations. These renovations were necessary to develop market spaces to suit the evolving needs of residents.

In the last few years, the Ministry of Heritage and Culture has taken notice of the critical situation of the Souq. This resulted in urgent intervention. The intervention started with the preparation of the necessary studies with the aim of carrying out the restoration work to make sure that the upgrades not only complemented the growth of economic movement in the Wilayat of Bahla but that the historical integrity of this site was preserved. The upgrades did not compromise the traditional appearance of the souk. Many tourists love the old architecture of the souk. The souk was visited by thousands of tourists last year. The tourists were buying many traditional items. They take the items back to their own countries. Dates were eaten by the tourists. They drank lots of Omani coffee.

What do these words and phrases from the text mean? Choose from the following list.

to make something less than it should be,   a very narrow road, a sticky mix of water and soil,   a usually extensive land area with a level surface raised sharply above adjacent land on at least one side,   come and take part in a process that is ongoing, bringing something back to its original condition,   to be in a place which has not changed over a long historical period of time, to maintain something in its original condition,   the bottom of something,   to make something of better quality,   the centre / middle of,   a rectangular stone used for building houses and other buildings,   complete and undivided / an undamaged condition,   a dangerous condition,   small rectangular stones used in building construction,   something which needs immediate attention,   a thing added to something to make it better,   a place

1.) lane _____

2.) transport back in time _____

3.) foot _____

4.) plateau _____

5.) mud _____

6.) brick _____

7.) concrete block _____

8.) heart of _____

9.) critical _____

10.) urgent _____

11.) intervention _____

12.) upgrade _____

13.) upgrade _____

14.) complement _____

15.) restoration _____

16.) integrity _____

17.) site _____

18.) preserve _____

19.) compromise _____

Answer these questions in complete sentences

1.) What makes the souks of Bahla a major tourist attraction?

_____

_____

2.) Where is the visitor to Bahla Souk transported to?

_____

_____

3.) Where is Bahla Souk located?

_____

_____

4.) What size of area is covered by the souk?

_____

_____

5.) How many shops does the souk include?

_____

_____

6.) What was the souk originally built with?

_____

_____

7.) What happened to some of the shops recently?

_____

_____

8.) What are the shops now made of?

_____

_____

9.) What has the souk seen?

_____

_____

10.) Why were the renovations necessary?

_____

_____

11.) What has the Ministry of Heritage and Culture taken notice of in the past few years?

_____

_____

Look at these sentences from the passage. If they are active, change them into the passive. If they are passive, change them into the passive.

1.) Many tourists love the old architecture of the souk.

_____

_____

2.) The souk was visited by thousands of tourists last year.

_____

_____

3.) The tourists were buying many traditional items.

_____

_____

4.) They take the items back to their own countries.

_____

_____

5.) Dates were eaten by the tourists.

_____

_____

6.) They drank lots of Omani coffee.

_____

_____

UNIT 5
Car Advertising

Some people sell cars by word of mouth, but you may not find too many buyers within your circle of friends and family. Advertising by word of mouth is free but not very effective. So it is necessary to advertise. There are a variety of places where you can advertise your car. Some ads, such as those in the newspaper, cost money, but others can be free.

There are a variety of markets wherein you can advertise the sale of your car. There are online classifieds such as Autobytel.com, Cars. com or Edmunds.com. These websites are specially designed for car sale advertisements.

Then there are the classified ads section of your local newspaper. Local weekly papers and free newspapers can often be found at supermarkets.

Then there are bulletin boards at supermarkets, libraries and college campuses

And then you can put a "For Sale" sign in the car's window. This should include your contact details.

What do these words and phrases from the text mean? Choose from the following list.

it does something well,   a place where you can read books and borrow books from,   things like your email address, telephone number etc,   someone who buys things,   telling people you have something to sell,   a part of something,   ads which are free or very cheap,   a newspaper that is sold in a limited geographical area – not all over the country,   the members of your family and your group of friends,   a board attached to a wall for pinning notices and advertisements on, something made in a special way for a specific purpose

   1.) advertising by word of mouth _____

       _____

   2.) effective _____

   3.) classified ads _____

   4.) bulletin boards _____

   5.) buyer _____

   6.) circle of family and friends _____

   7.) specially designed _____

   8.) section _____

   9.) library _____

   10.) contact details _____

   11.) local newspaper _____

Answer these questions in complete sentences

1.) What kind of advertising will not be very effective in selling your car?

_____

_____

2.) Is advertising in the newspapers free?

_____

_____

3.) What are the two websites mentioned in the text?

_____

_____

4.) What are they specially designed for?

_____

_____

5.) Where are the classified ads?

_____

_____

6.) What can be found at supermarkets.

_____

_____

7.) Where can bulletin boards be found?

_____

_____

8.) Where can a "For Sale" sign be put?

_____

_____

9.) What does a "For Sale" sign tell people?

_____

_____

10.) What should you include in the "For Sale" sign?

_____

_____

Owned the car: 6 years
Use of the car: Every day
Repaired: Three times
Accidents: 5
Petrol usage: 20 miles to the gallon
Drivers: His friends drive the car.
Vehicle servicing: Every year
Car cleaning: Once a month
Bought: 2010
Paid: $58,000
Done: 50,000 kilometers

Johnny Swindler is selling his car. He is talking to a potential buyer on the phone. Johnny Swindler is not telling the truth about the car. Look at the information above and correct Johnny's sentences.

Example: I paid $68,000 for the car.

He didn't pay $68,000 for the car. He paid $58,000 for it

1.) I bought it in 2019.

_____

_____

2.) It has only done 20,000 kilometres.

_____

_____

3.) I have owned the car for only one year.

_____

_____

4.) I have used the car only at weekends.

_____

_____

5.) It has been repaired once.

_____

_____

6.) I have never had any accidents with the car.

_____

_____

7.) The car gives you 40 miles to the gallon.

_____

_____

8.) I am the only driver.

_____

_____

9.) The car is serviced every six months.

_____

_____

10.) The car was cleaned once a week.

_____

_____

READING FOR ENJOYMENT
Advertising Children's Toys

I remember when I was a child waking up early on Saturday mornings and sitting down in front of the TV to watch all the children's programmes. I remember the advertisements for all kinds of toys and games. And I remember how I begged my parents to buy me these amazing toys.

In those days what you saw on TV and in the newspapers were the only places you saw these ads for toys and games. Just like adults, kids are being constantly shown ads online as well as on the TV. Children are impressionable, and so there needs to be ethics on how businesses advertise to children in the modern world. If part of a company's target audience includes children, here are some ethical guidelines businesses need to follow to maintain the trust of their consumers.

Advertisers should not fool children into thinking that they "need" a product. This often happens on mobile devices. Often, <u>parents use tablets and phones to entertain kids</u> when they are busy. There is a whole market of apps to teach and play with kids, but all of these have ads of some kind. Since kids are often on these devices with little or no supervision, some devious app developers include ads that either force kids to click on them and buy items with their parent's money and without their parents' consent, or just make it too hard to exit the ad.

If at any time a business is lying to children about a product, business strategy should be reconsidered. Not only is it immoral to fail to tell the truth, the company will damage its business' reputation with adults — the people who actually have the money.

Answer the following questions in complete sentences

1.) What does the author of the text remember doing when he was a child?

2.) What were the advertisements that he saw for?

3.) Whom did he beg to buy him the goods that were advertised?

4.) Apart from the TV and newspapers, where do children see ads?

5.) Why do companies need to be ethical in their advertisements to children?

_____

_____

6.) What do parents do to keep their children entertained when they are busy?

_____

_____

7.) Whose money do the children use to buy items they see on tablets and phones?

_____

_____

8.) What is it immoral for companies to do?

_____

_____

9.) Who will the company damage its reputation with if it does not change its strategy?

_____

_____

10.) Who actually has the money?

_____

_____

THEME 18

AFTER SCHOOL

UNIT 1
Leaving school / starting university

Revision: present perfect active.

My names is Abdullah Mansour. I am an engineering student at Sohar University. I have been at this university for three years. In another two years I will graduate. I have just completed an essay. I have given the essay to my lecturer. He has told me to give it to him. I have done a lot today. I have read a chapter of an engineering textbook. I have listened to a lecture. I have phoned my parents. My friend Ali has asked me to go to a football match with him.

The present perfect passive. The words in *italics* are where the above paragraph has been changed into the passive voice.

My name is Abdullah Mansour. I am an engineering student at Sohar University. I have been at this university for three years. In another two years I will graduate. *An essay has just been completed by me. My lecturer has just been given the essay to by me. I have been told by him to give it to him. A lot of things have been done by me today. A chapter of an engineering book has been read by me. A lecture has been listened to by me. My parents have been phoned by me. I have been asked by my friend Ali to go to a football match with him.*

Change the following paragraph from the present perfect active into the present perfect passive.

I have just repaired my brother's car. He has had this car for 15 years. He has driven it for 15 years. I have changed the oil. I have put in new spark plugs. I have adjusted the gear lever. I have corrected the steering. My brother has given me the ignition keys of his car. He has asked me to test drive it. I have told him I will do that later.

Read

I had thought university life was all fun and games. I had got myself ready for an easy time there, but the reality was quite different — a demanding workload, strict deadlines and the realisation that I needed a lot of mental, emotional and physical strength.

With the wisdom of hindsight, there are a lot of things I wish I had done differently when I was at university. I had been quite proud of my high school score and felt the need to tell everyone about it, but no one either listened or cared.

You might have thought that your whole future depends on that score, but it really means very little in the scheme of things at university.

It is important to read a lot, observe a lot and learn a lot to expose yourself to as many different fields as possible.

The more you know about the world, the more you will find out what career options there are out there for you.

Actively expanding your knowledge is another way to figure out what you're really interested in. One of the things I had personally taken for granted during my time at uni was the library — more specifically my ability to access academic papers for free! Once you graduate you have to pay to get access to these papers.

Finding new and interesting people to introduce to your existing friends could also have other benefits that go beyond socialising, like establishing the foundation for a strong professional network. This is important for career development when university is finished. Had I used my time wisely at university? I think I had used my time wisely at university. But I often think I could have done better. My friends often think they could have done better too.

What do these words and phrases from the text mean? Choose from the following list.

good sense / being able to make a good judgement,   to look at something,   to show to everyone,   number of people connected to your business or profession,   a lot of work to do, in a university it means a subject,   when a piece of work must be finished / no later,   possibilities for different kinds of jobs, to be very pleased with yourself because of an achievement,   to solve a problem,   the way a system is set up,   to consider something as normal and can be obtained with no effort,   to see something in the past looking at it in the present

1.) demanding workload _____

2.) strict deadlines _____

3.) wisdom _____

4.) hindsight _____

5.) proud _____

6.) scheme of things _____

7.) observe _____

8.) observe _____

9.) expose _____

10.) field _____

11.) career options _____

12.) figure out _____

13.) take for granted _____

14.) professional network _____

Answer these questions in complete sentences

1.) What had the writer of the text thought about university life?

_____

_____

2.) What had he got himself ready for?

_____

_____

3.) Explain how the reality of university life was different to how he had imagined it to be.

_____

_____

4.) What does the writer wish he had done with the wisdom of hindsight?

_____

_____

5.) What had he been quite proud of?

_____

_____

6.) What had the writer taken for granted when he was at university?

_____

_____

7.) What do you have to pay for when you graduate?

_____

_____

8.) What does the writer think he had done?

_____

_____

9.) What does he often think

_____

_____

10.) What do his friends often think?

_____

_____

UNIT 2
The first few days at university

The first few days at university can be the most difficult in your whole time at university. It was for me. I had been dropped at the halls of residence by the university bus. After I had taken my luggage to my room, I wanted to find out as much as possible before the start of the academic year. Before I arrived at university, I had been informed where to go by an email from those responsible for assisting freshman students. I had been told by the main reception to go and have a discussion with my academic advisor.

I had an interesting discussion with my advisor. After that I went back to my room in the halls of residence. After my suitcases had been unpacked, I decided to tidy up the room. A bed, a table, and a chair had been put in the room and there were curtains on the window. No pictures had been hung on the walls, so I put up some of my own.

I then went outside and started walking around the campus. It is a good idea to get to know the campus. I had been given a map of the campus by the university's main reception. I used it to locate where various places were: shops, restaurants, laundries, pharmacies, the post office and medical facilities. I had been told by older students that everything I needed was on the campus.

When I had been familiarised with the campus, I decided to extend my exploration to the wider township. I identified the theatres, the cinemas, the restaurants and the bookshops.

I am so glad that I made the effort to find out as much as I could about the university and the town. Now that I had been made aware of the facilities available to me both on and off campus, I felt more confident that I could settle down to my academic pursuits.

What do these words and phrases from paragraphs 1 &2 of the text mean? Choose from the following list.

a first year student at a college or university, your suitcases and other containers used for traveling with your personal belongings, the buildings where students live when they are at university, past of hang / to suspend something from a height, a college year of study, to make a place clean, help, the bus stops and lets you get off, take everything out of a suitcase, a member of faculty who tells you what the best courses are for you, a talk

1.) dropped off by the bus _____

_____

2.) halls of residence _____

3.) luggage _____

4.) academic year _____

5.) assist _____

6.) freshman _____

7.) academic advisor _____

8.) discussion _____

9.) unpack a suitcase _____

10.) tidy up _____

11.) hung _____

Answer the following questions in complete sentences

1.) Where had the writer been dropped by the university bus?

_____

_____

2.) What had the writer taken to his room?

_____

_____

3.) What had the writer been informed about before he arrived at university?

_____

_____

4.) What had he been told to do by the main reception?

_____

_____

5.) What had happened to the writer's suitcases?

_____

_____

6.) What had been put in the room?

_____

_____

7.) What had not been hung on the walls?

_____

_____

What do these words and phrases from paragraphs 3 &5 of the text mean? Choose from the following list.

get to know things,   a place in an organisation which greets visitors and welcomes them,   courses you do at an educational institution,   finish what you are doing and be relaxed,   a kind of diagram to show you where places are,   a place where you can wash clothes,   you are sure you can do something successfully,   the area of a town,   a place where you can buy stamps and send letters,   a place where you can watch films on a big screen,   looking around trying to discover new things, a place where actors perform plays on a stage,   an outlet where you can buy medicines

1.) reception _____

2.) map_____

3.) laundry_____

4.) pharmacy _____

5.) post office _____

6.) familiarise _____

7.) exploration _____

8.) township _____

9.) theatre _____

10.) cinema _____

11.) feel confident _____

12.)settle down _____

13.)academic pursuits _____

Answer the following questions in complete sentences

1.) What had the writer been given by the university's main reception?

_____

_____

2.) What had the writer been told by older students?

_____

_____

3.) What had he been familiarised with?

_____

_____

4.) What had he been made aware of?

_____

_____

Change the following sentences from the past perfect active to the past perfect passive.

Example: My brother had eaten the cake.

The cake had been eaten by my brother.

1.) The cat had drunk all the milk.

_____

_____

2.) The cleaners hadn't cleaned the rooms.

_____

_____

3.) Had the student written the essay?

_____

_____

4.) Professor Smith had delivered a lecture.

_____

_____

5.) The drivers hadn't parked the cars.

_____

_____

6.) The engineers hadn't fixed the machine.

_____

_____

7.) Had the visitors seen the garden?

_____

_____

8.) The customers had bought the newspapers.

_____

_____

9.) The lorries had delivered the chickens.

_____

_____

10.) Jim Barry had published a book?

_____

_____

Change the following sentences from the past perfect passive into the past perfect active

Example: The tea had been brought by the waiter.

The waiter had brought the tea.

1.) The workers had been given jobs by the factory.

_____

_____

2.) The nest had been built by the birds.

_____

_____

3.) Had the car been cleaned by John?

_____

_____

4.) The tin of soup hadn't been opened by me.

_____

_____

5.) The television hadn't been broken by Bobby.

_____

_____

6.) Had the computer been rebooted by you?

_____

_____

7.) Had the dinner been prepared by the chef?

_____

_____

8.) The film hadn't been seen by him.

_____

_____

9.) The money hadn't been counted by the accountant.

_____

_____

10.) Tim had been ordered by the boss to phone the client.

_____

_____

UNIT 3
Studying abroad

Some Omani students like to study abroad. There are many advantages in doing this. They can learn a new language, they can taste different types of cuisine and they can experience new cultures. However, there is a downside to all of this. Omani students usually face a number of challenges in the country in which they choose to study.

First of all, they are away from their families. Jasim went to the United States to study Pharmacy. He speaks of his experience there: "At first I felt like an outsider. It was difficult to make any friends. When I was with a group of other students, I didn't understand what they were talking about. When they told a joke, I didn't laugh because I didn't understand the joke. However all the students I had met who came from other countries, had the same problems as I had. After some time I got accustomed to the different culture.

"Then there were the language difficulties. English had been taught to me at school but I was still deficient in it when I reached the US. Nevertheless, I quickly learned a lot of English as I had to speak it all day and every day. Actually, I learned more English in my first month in the US than I had learned over many years at school.

"I also had to deal with a different currency. In Oman we use riyals but in America they use dollars. And then there was being far from my family. In Oman, when we have problems, we go to our families for help. I kept in touch with my family through telephonic contact and the social media, but this was not the same as being near them."

What do these words and phrases from the text mean? Choose from the following list.

handle / use,   being in another country,   to look at and see which is challenging,   maintain contact,   a disadvantage, contact by phone,   money,   someone from another place, however,   saying something funny,   not enough of

1.) abroad _____

2.) downside _____

3.) face _____

4.) outsider _____

5.) joke _____

6.) deficient _____

7.) nevertheless _____

8.) currency _____

9.) deal with _____

10.) keep in touch _____

11.) telephonic contact _____

Answer these questions in complete sentences

1.) Where do some Omani students like to study?

_____

_____

2.) What do some Omani students face in the country in which they choose to study?

_____

_____

3.) Which country did Jasim go to to study?

_____

_____

4.) What did he feel like at first?

_____

_____

5.) Which subject did he study?

_____

_____

6.) Why didn't Jasim laugh at the jokes?

_____

_____

7.) Who had the same problems as Jasim?

_____

_____

8.) What currency do they use in America?

_____

_____

9.) Where do Omanis go to for help when they have problems?

_____

_____

10.) How did Jasim keep in touch with his family?

_____

_____

Change these sentences from the active to the passive forms

1.) I feed the cat every day.

_____

_____

2.) The painters are painting the walls.

_____

_____

3.) John gave Maria a box of chocolates.

_____

_____

4.) Billy was repairing the bicycle.

_____

_____

5.) I have seen the patient

_____

_____

6.) Player Number Six had scored a goal.

_____

_____

7.) Was he driving a car last night?

_____

_____

8.) Do you often bake cakes?

_____

_____

9.) Did you lock the door?

_____

_____

10.) He hadn't finished the job.

_____

_____

UNIT 4
Which subject should you choose at college?

When students leave school and go to university, they are faced with having to choose their major. Although they will have to study a number of subjects, they will have to specialise in one. So what is the criteria for choice of major?

There are a few things that students will have to take into consideration when thinking about their field of specialisation. First and foremost, they must think what their strongest area is – languages, history, science, maths, engineering, medicine, law and so forth.

Next, they have to think about career prospects in their chosen major. They should find out from those who have already graduated what the job market conditions are. It is very important to seek the advice of graduates who now have to find employment related to their degree.

It is a good idea for students to make a right choice of university. Some universities are noted for being strong in some subjects but not in others. When a student has set his mind on a university, he should find out what the prerequisite qualifications are for entering that university. If the prerequisites are high, then the student should look at other universities in case he does not meet the prerequisite standards for his first choice. If the student is a non-native speaker of English, he should find out what the university requires in TOEFL or IELTS scores if he is applying for a foreign university place.

Finally, it is important to examine the location of the university. Is it very far from home? Does it have sufficient facilities for everyday life? It might even be a good idea to visit the university to check out its facilities.

It is very important to make the right choice of major and the right choice of university. The student will spend the next three or four years of his life not only studying at but living at the university of his choice. The student should be happy with his choice.

What do these words and phrases from the text mean? Choose from the following list.

qualifications you need prior to entry into a job or college,   the most important of all,   the subject you will graduate in,   from another country,   connected to,   a rule or a standard against which you evaluate something,   a person whose first language is not English,   the subject area you will study the most intensely,   renowned for / famous for,   the chances of finding a job,   to make a strong and final choice,   look for

1.) major _____

2.) criteria _____

3.) field of specialisation _____

4.) first and foremost _____

5.) career prospects _____

6.) seek _____

7.) related to _____

8.) noted for _____

9.) set your mind on something _____

10.) prerequisite qualifications _____

11.) non-native speaker of English _____

12.) foreign _____

Answer these questions in complete sentences

1.) What are students faced with before they go to university?

_____

_____

2.) How many subjects will students specialise in at university?

_____

_____

3.) What is the first and foremost thing students must think about in their chosen major?

_____

_____

4.) What must students find out from those who have already graduated in their chosen field of specialisation?

_____

_____

5.) What are some universities noted for?

_____

_____

6.) What should non-native speakers of English find out?

_____

_____

7.) What should a student do once he has set his mind on a particular university?

_____

_____

8.) Why should a student visit a university before joining it?

_____

_____

9.) How many years will a student live and study at a university?

_____

_____

10.) What should the student be happy with?

_____

_____

Change these sentences. If a sentence is active, change it to passive. If a sentence is passive, change it to active.

1.) I have eaten the sandwich.

_____

_____

2.) The street has been tarred by the road-workers.

_____

_____

3.) Johnny has bought an apple.

_____

_____

4.) Have you seen the latest film?

_____

_____

5.) The coffee hasn't been made by Jane yet?

_____

_____

6.) The teacher is instructing the students.

_____

_____

7.) The children were blowing up the balloons.

_____

_____

8.) The money was being counted by the manager.

_____

_____

9.) The burglar had broken into the building.

_____

_____

10.) The driver had been stopped by the police.

_____

_____

UNIT 5
Learning a foreign language

Learning a foreign language is hard work. But if you persevere with it, you will find that there are many advantages.

As our brains work out the meaning of a foreign language, we develop key learning skills such as cognitive thinking and problem-solving. Well-developed critical thinking skills are a significant benefit both personally and in professions.

Learning a language enhances your memory. This means that multilingual people have brains that are stronger. They are quick to recall a plethora of information such as names, directions, facts, and figures.

People who have developed the ability to think in different languages and move from one to the other become more competent multi-taskers.

A study from Spain's University of Pompeu Fabra revealed that multilingual people are better at observing their surroundings. They easily spot anything that is irrelevant or deceptive. They're also better at spotting misleading information. The study was conducted comparing multilingual and monolingual subjects and the former notably had the edge over the latter.

According to a study from the University of Chicago, multilingual people are better at decision making.

Learning a new language also makes you a better listener as you have to try to understand the meaning of the foreign lexical items.

As a result of higher cognitive skills produced by language learning, studies show that the benefits of learning a new language include higher scores on exams in maths, reading comprehension and vocabulary by multilingual students compared to the scores of monolingual students.

According to Eton Institute (September 2014), 89% of employers stated that multilingual employees add value to the workforce and 88% stated that recruiting team members with language skills is important to their company. Having more than one language definitely gives prospective employees a competitive edge in the modern world.

What do these words and phrases from the text mean? Choose from the following list.

you can speak only one language, analyzing facts to form a judgement, to know how to do something, to see/ to notice, the second noun mentioned without a connective meaning, an advantage I competition, having the ability to speak more than one language, not true / lies, things around you, a single word or part of a word in a language, possible / expected, to keep on doing something / not to give up, to have an advantage, the first noun mentioned, get knowledge through experience / and through thought / and through sensory input, worth, information that takes you in the wrong direction, research / investigation, important

FRANCIS A. ANDREW

skills needed for the learning process,   doing different things at the same time,   lots of something,   a career which requires highly skilled knowledge and abilities,   to hire someone / to give them a job

1.) ability _____

2.) preserve _____

3.) key learning skills _____

4.) cognitive thinking _____

5.) critical thinking _____

6.) multi-task _____

7.) plethora _____

8.) a study _____

9.) multilingual _____

10.) surroundings _____

11.) spot _____

12.) irrelevant _____

13.) deceptive _____

14.) misleading information _____

15.) monolingual _____

16.) to have the edge over _____

17.) lexical item _____

18.) value _____

19.) prospective _____

20.)competitive edge _____

21.) profession _____

22.)the former _____

23.)the latter _____

24.)recruit _____

1.) What key learning skills do we develop when working out the meaning of a foreign language?

_____

_____

2.) What does learning a language do for your memory?

_____

_____

3.) From which university was the study which showed that multilingual people are better at observing their surroundings?

_____

_____

4.) Who were compared in the study?

_____

_____

5.) Who exactly are the former and who are the latter in the text?

_____

_____

6.) What did the University of Chicago's study show?

_____

_____

7.) In what other subjects does learning a new language produce better results?

_____

_____

8.) What did the Eton Institute find out about eight nine percent of employers?

_____

_____

9.) What did eighty eight percent of employers say about recruiting people with linguistic ability?

_____

_____

10.) What does having more than one language give prospective employees?

_____

_____

Change these present tense verbs into their past tense equivalents

1.) Mother cooks the dinner.

_____

_____

2.) I am installing a programme in the computer.

_____

_____

3.) The living-room is being painted by John and Peter.

_____

_____

4.) The house has been sold.

_____

_____

5.) The baker has baked some bread,

_____

_____

6.) You are being given the results of your exam.

_____

_____

7.) They drink a lot of tea.

_____

_____

8.) The cakes aren't made by Billy.

_____

_____

9.) Are they playing football?

_____

_____

10.) They haven't driven that car.

_____

_____

READING FOR ENJOYMENT
The Eskimo People

Eskimo, any member of a group of peoples who, with the closely related <u>Aleuts</u>, <u>constitute</u> the chief element in the <u>indigenous</u> population of the <u>Arctic</u> and subarctic regions of <u>Greenland</u>, <u>Canada</u>, the <u>United States</u>, and far eastern Russia (<u>Siberia</u>). Early 21st-century population estimates indicated more than 135,000 individuals of Eskimo descent, with some 85,000 living in <u>North America</u>, 50,000 in Greenland, and the remainder in Siberia.

Eskimo peoples vary with their languages and <u>dialects</u>. They include such names as Inuit, Inupiat, <u>Yupik</u>, and Alutiit, each of which is a regional variant meaning "the people" or "the real people." The name Eskimo, which has been applied to Arctic peoples by Europeans and others since the 16th century, originated with the <u>Innu</u> (Montagnais), a group of <u>Algonquian speakers</u>; once <u>erroneously</u> thought to mean "eaters of <u>raw flesh</u>," the name is now believed to make reference to <u>snowshoes</u>.

One of the oldest known Eskimo archaeological sites was found on Saglek Bay, <u>Labrador</u>, and dates to approximately 3,800 years ago.

Another was found on Umnak Island in the Aleutians, for which an age of approximately 3,000 years was recorded.

Culturally, traditional Eskimo life was totally adapted to an extremely cold, snow- and icebound environment in which vegetable foods were almost nonexistent, trees were scarce, and caribou, seal, walrus, and whale meat, whale blubber, and fish were the major food sources. Eskimo people used harpoons to kill seals, which they hunted either on the ice or from kayaks, skin-covered, one-person canoes.

Whales were hunted by using larger boats called umiaks. In the summer most Eskimo families hunted caribou and other land animals with bows and arrows. Dogsleds were the basic means of transport on land. Eskimo clothing was fashioned of caribou furs, which provided protection against the extreme cold. Most Eskimo wintered in either snow-block houses called igloos or semisubterranean houses built of stone or sod over wooden or whalebone frameworks. In summer many Eskimo lived in animal-skin tents. Their basic social and economic unit was the nuclear family.

Eskimo life has changed greatly because of increased contact with societies to the south. Snowmobiles have generally replaced dogs for land transport, and rifles have replaced harpoons for hunting purposes. Outboard motors, store-bought clothing, and numerous other manufactured items have entered the culture, and money, unknown in the traditional Eskimo economy, has become a necessity.

Many Eskimo have abandoned nomadic hunting and now live in northern towns and cities, often working in mines and oil fields. Others, particularly in Canada, have formed cooperatives to market their handicrafts, fish catches, and tourism ventures. The creation of Nunavut, a new Canadian territory, in 1999 helped to support a revitalization of traditional indigenous culture in North America.

Answer the questions in complete sentences

1.) In which parts of the world do the Eskimos live?

_____

_____

2. How many Eskimos live in North America?

_____

_____

3.) Where was one of the oldest Eskimo archaeological sites found?

_____

_____

4.) How far back does it date?

_____

_____

5.) How old is the Eskimo archaeological site of Umnak Island?

_____

_____

6.) When did the Eskimo hunt caribou?

_____

_____

7.) What kind of food is non-existent for the Eskimo?

_____

_____

8.) What kind of boats were used for hunting whales?

_____

_____

9.) What are the snow-block houses of the Eskimo called?

_____

_____

10.) Where do many Eskimos work now?

_____

_____

THEME 19

HOTELS, FOOD AND TOURISM IN OMAN AND

UNIT 1
Dishes of Oman

Revision: Conditional Type 1 sentences

Sameer and Mansour are talking about what they want to do. However, whether or not they can do these things depends on a number of things.

S: If my father gives me ten riyals, I'll buy a book.

M: Which book would you like to buy, Sameer?

S: I will buy a book on interesting tourist sites in Oman if the bookshop has these kinds of books.

M: Why do you want to read a book on tourist sites?

S: If I successfully pass my exams, I will go into the tourist business.

M: If the rain stops, I will play football.

S: You play a lot of football, Mansour.

M: If my football skills improve, I'll apply to join a professional football club.

S: If you are accepted, will you play in the national team?

M: If I become a really good player, I will try to play in the national team.

Answer these questions using the first conditional

1.) What will Sameer do if his father gives him ten riyals?

_____

_____

2.) What book will he buy if the bookshop has these kinds of books?

_____

_____

3.) What will Sameer do if he successfully passes his exams?

_____

_____

4.) What will Mansour do if the rain stops?

_____

_____

5.) What will he do if his football skills improve?

_____

_____

6.) What will he do if he becomes a really good player?

_____

_____

Read

Biryani is a traditional dish of Oman. There are basically two types of biryani – chicken biryani and lamb biryani.

If you want to prepare this mouth-watering chicken biryani recipe, you will have to marinate the chicken. To do this, take a large bowl and add Greek yoghurt in it along with turmeric, chili powder along with salt as per your taste in a small bowl. Mix well using a spoon and then, add the chicken thighs. If you keep aside for about 20-30 minutes, the yogurt mixture will be properly absorbed by the chicken. Also, soak saffron in the milk to make saffron milk and keep aside.

In the meantime, pour refined oil in a deep-bottomed pan, keeping it on medium flame. Add cumin seeds and green cardamom in it and saute for about 2 minutes. Once done, immediately add the sliced onion and fry for 2-3 minutes straight. Make sure you don't burn it, so when the onion starts to get brown in colour, add tomatoes and tomato puree and fry for another 5 minutes.

Next, add the slit green chilies to the mixture along with ginger-garlic paste, frying the mixture yet again for a minute. Then, add coriander powder and turn the flame to medium-low while stirring and cooking the masala. If you quickly add the marinated chicken and mix for a while the ingredients will absorb the juices properly.

Turn the flame to medium again and heat-through for about 5-6 minutes only and then turn it over to low heat. Cover with a lid and let simmer for 5 minutes. If you don't keep stirring during the entire process, the chicken might stick to the bottom, eventually ending up burnt. You can add little water, if you find it too thick.

Once done, turn off the flame and add half of the boiled rice in the pan and keep the rest aside until required. Sprinkle milk soaked saffron along with garam masala, mint and coriander leaves. Put the remaining rice over this layer and garnish with the same four ingredients.

Lastly, cover the lid, turn the flame to low medium and let the rice cook for about 5 minutes. Once done, put it off and let the biryani stay covered for about another 10 minutes. Serve hot, along with raita or any chutney of your choice.

What do these words and phrases from paragraphs 1, 2 & 3 mean? Choose from the following list.

cook using oil, delicious / tasty, to take in something (usually a liquid) through tiny openings, instructions on how to cook something, cut something into very thin pieces, cooking something with a small amount of oil in a shallow pan, to put (food, such as meat or fish) in a sauce for some time to add flavour or tenderise, the foreleg, something mashed to a paste, a shallow cooking vessel, a deep dish, the visible coloured part of a fire

1.) mouth-watering _____

2.) recipe _____

3.) marinate _____

4.) bowl _____

5.) thigh _____

6.) absorb _____

7.) pan _____

8.) flame _____

9.) sliced _____

10.) puree _____

11.) fry _____

Answer these questions in complete sentences

1.) How many types of biryani are there?

_____

_____

2.) What will you first have to do to the chicken before you make chicken biryani?

_____

_____

3.) What will happen if you keep aside the mix for twenty to thirty minutes?

_____

_____

4.) What must you make sure about the onion?

_____

_____

What do these words and phrases from paragraphs 4 -7 mean? Choose from the following list.

a piece placed over an open container,   something which has had too much heat,   something which is holding tightly to a surface,   to cook something in a liquid slowly until it gives off steam,   to move a liquid around in a circular direction,   to scatter tiny pieces of something over another thing,   a thing you need to make food,   put something over the top of another thing,   a level of material on top of another material,   very fine tiny particles

1.) stir _____

2.) powder _____

3.) cover _____

4.) lid _____

5.) simmer _____

6.) stick _____

7.) burnt _____

8.) sprinkle _____

9.) layer _____

10.) ingredient _____

Answer the following questions in complete sentences

1.) How will the ingredients absorb the juices quickly?

_____

_____

2.) What will happen if you don't keep stirring for the entire process?

_____

_____

3.) How should the biryani be served?

_____

_____

Make sentences in the first conditional using the words given

Example: John / get job / buy car

If John gets a job, he will buy a car.

1.) I / go / Paris / see Eifel Tower

_____

_____

2.) Ahmed / passes / his exams / be very happy

_____

_____

3.) our team / score / another goal /we win the match

_____

_____

4.) you / phone / hotel / be able to reserve a room

_____

_____

5.) Tony / doesn't go /on a diet / get fat

_____

_____

6.) tell me the name of the book / I /buy / for you

_____

_____

7.) people / watch TV too much / damage their eyes

_____

_____

8.) Jonny / finish / his homework / play football

_____

_____

9.) students / read / a lot of books / gain a lot of knowledge

_____

_____

10.) you / don't get / enough sleep / get very tired

_____

_____

UNIT 2
Eating out in Salalah

Revision: The simple future tense active and passive

Simple future tense in the active voice

I will be very busy tomorrow. I will take the car to the workshop. I will ask the mechanics to repair it. After that, I will withdraw money from the bank. Then I will buy a new washing machine. Next, I will eat dinner in a restaurant. After I have eaten dinner, I will send some emails. I will then discuss some business matters with the bank manager. Finally, I will read the daily newspaper. Then I will go home.

The simple future tense in the passive voice. The words in *italics* **are where the above paragraph has been changed into the passive voice.**

I will be very busy tomorrow. *The car will be taken to the workshop by me. The mechanics will be asked to repair it. After that, money will be withdrawn from the banks. Then a new washing machine will be bought. Dinner will be eaten in a restaurant.* After I have eaten dinner, *some emails will be sent. Some business matters will be discussed by the bank manager and me. Finally, the daily newspaper will be read by me.* Then I will go home.

FRANCIS A. ANDREW

Read the following passage which is written in the future simple active. Then rewrite it using the future simple passive.

The warehouse workers will be busy all day tomorrow. John will do the stocktaking and Mary will record the stock. Bill will drive the forklift truck and he will lift some things on to the shelves. The electricians will check the lights. The IT people will reboot all the computers. The manager and the assistant manager will rearrange the storage system in the warehouse. They will open a new section of the warehouse.

_____

_____

_____

_____

_____

_____

_____

_____

Read

Mekong in Al Baleed resort by Anantara brings you the best of Asian cuisines, more specifically those of Vietnam, Thailand, and China. The restaurant has an indoor and terrace area to enjoy al fresco evenings overlooking the romantic lagoon. Each dish is cooked following the centuries-old recipes and the restaurant quickly became famous in Salalah. If you enjoy beef dishes, be sure to try the beef pho soup, papaya salad and shaking beef!

If you like not just eating out but eating outside the Dolphin beach restaurant will be for you. It features a white sand beach and has a tropical appearance. It overlooks the Indian Ocean. Savour some salad, sandwiches or a burger during the day and enjoy a themed dinner in the evening. From seafood to Lebanese buffet, you will get to taste specialties from around the world each day. Relax with a traditional shisha, or a private tent for families.

If you want to get out of the classy hotel restaurants and try the best Lebanese restaurant in Oman, Baalbeck is the best place for you to go to. With simple decor, the restaurant serves the best Lebanese specialties such as hummus, baba ganoush, kebabs and much more! A black tea is offered at the end of your meal, as this is Arabic hospitality! All ingredients are got fresh every day and you might see the restaurant's owners buying seafood at the fish market to serve you only the freshest fish for dinner!

What do these words and phrases from the text mean? Choose from the following list.

posh / very decorative,   something that looks like it is from the tropics,   exciting /mysterious / unusual,   fish just caught from the sea or a river,   an inlet of sea water with land on each side,   eat slowly so as to enjoy the taste

1.) romantic _____

2.) lagoon _____

3.) tropical appearance _____

4.) savour _____

5.) classy _____

6.) fresh fish _____

Answer the following questions in complete sentences

1.) What is brought to you by Mekong?

2.) How is each dish cooked?

3.) What does this restaurant overlook?

4.) What will you try if you enjoy beef dishes?

5.) Which restaurant do you go to if you want to eat outside?

6.) What kind of an appearance does the Dolphin Restaurant have?

7.) What does the restaurant provide for families?

8.) Where will you go if you want Lebanese food?

_____

_____

9.) What is offered at the end of your meal in Baalbeck Restaurant?

_____

_____

10.) What can you say about the fish they serve you at this restaurant?

_____

_____

UNIT 3
Hotels in Dubai

Dubai leads in the world's highest hotel occupancy rates. In 2006, the Dubai hotel occupancy rate was 86%, the highest ever in Dubai.

In 1993, the city had 167 hotels with 9,383 rooms, while the number shot up to 272 hotels and doubled the number of rooms to 23,170 in 2002. In 2005, it increased to 28,999 rooms. In 2008, the hotel rooms jumped to 43,419, with 6,105,813 hotel guests and a 70 percent occupancy rate. In 2009, the number of hotel rooms increased to 58,188. In 2010, it jumped to 67,369 rooms, an increase of 9,181 in one year due to the massive rise in visitor arrivals. Dubai hosted a record 10 million visitors in 2012, an increase of 9.3% from the previous year.

In 2013 more than 32,686 hotel rooms were planned, including 17,162 hotel rooms which were under construction. Thirty new hotels opened in 2010. In January 2010, the occupancy rate was at 81 percent, the second highest ever for Dubai; however, throughout the year, the occupancy rate settled at 71 percent, an increase of one percent from 2009. The city's hotels experienced a decline of 4.2 percent in revenue per available room (RevPAR), which reached $154 million in 2010.

If you go to Dubai, you will find lots of hotels. If you want to be sure of a room, you will have to book in advance. If you book in advance, you will have to pay a deposit.

What do these words and phrases from the text mean? Choose from the following list.

the number of room in a hotel with guests in them,   2x,   to make a reservation prior to my arrival at the hotel,   all during the year,   income,   increase sharply to a higher number,   to reduce / fall,   very big / huge / enormous

1.) occupancy rate _____

2.) doubled _____

3.) jumped to _____

4.) massive _____

5.) throughout the year _____

6.) decline _____

7.) revenue _____

8.) book in advance _____

Answer the questions in complete sentences

1.) What was the occupancy rate for Dubai hotels in 1986?

_____

_____

2.) What was the total number of hotel rooms in Dubai in 1993?

_____

_____

3.) In which year did Dubai have twenty eight thousand and nine hundred and ninety nine rooms?

_____

_____

4.) How many visitors did Dubai host in 2012?

_____

_____

5.) What rate of increase was this from 2011?

_____

_____

6.) How many hotel rooms were planned in 2013?

_____

_____

7.) In which year did thirty new hotels open?

_____

_____

8.) What will I find if I go to Dubai?

_____

_____

9.) What will I have to do if I want to be sure of a room?

_____

_____

10.) What will I have to do if I want to book in advance?

_____

_____

You are giving advice to a friend. Use the words to make first conditional sentences.

Example: fat / eat / too much

You will get fat if you eat too much.

Example: your teacher / get angry / no do / homework

Your teacher will get angry if you don't do your homework

1.) no book/ hotel in advance in Dubai /no get room

_____

_____

2.) tea in hotel room / have to call Room service

_____

_____

3.) want your room key / have to ask Reception

_____

_____

4.) you want a tour of Dubai / have to hire a tour guide

_____

_____

5.) go straight ahead / find lifts

_____

_____

Change these sentences from the future simple active to the future simple passive

1.) I will make some tea at three o'clock.

_____

_____

2.) John will visit us tomorrow.

_____

_____

3.) The owners will refurbish the hotel.

_____

_____

4.) The secretary will book the hotel room tomorrow morning.

_____

_____

5.) The doctor will examine the patient in ten minutes.

UNIT 4
Tourist sites in Yemen

Socotra Island is a very well-known destination for the visitors to Yemen. Yemen has some very unusually shaped trees called bottle trees. They are short and stocky and grow in the rocky regions. If you travel to the rocky regions, you will see those strange looking trees. The trunks of these trees are stout near the ground and slender near the top. This is why they are called bottle trees. Tourists will be amazed by them.

The ancient city of Sanaa is located in downtown Sanaa. It has a wide variety of awesome views. The city has been inhabited for more than 2,000 years and has a sensational concoction of old houses with beautiful architecture.

Taiz is a little, but photogenic and amazing mountain village in southwest Yemen, where you can find the marvelous Al-Qahira Fortress. This is one of the most captivating and renowned destinations for tourists. It is situated on an elevated rocky peak. If you stand at the base of the fort, you will discover that the panoramic views from there are wonderful.

Al Mukalla Harbour is the key seaport of Yemen and is situated in the center of the southern coastline of the country. It is a completely bustling harbour, which is filled mainly with the tiny fishing boats, though some larger vessels sometimes dock there. If you go there, you will find that Al Mukalla Harbour is one of the most amazing spots in all of Yemen. Within the town there are many, stores, eateries, and souks.

What do these words and phrases from paragraphs 1 & 2 of the text mean? Choose from the following list.

places where there are lots of rocks and stones,   slim / thin,   a mixture of different things,   people live there,   wonderful / amazing,   the long main part of a tree,   well built and strong, astonishing,   fat,   in the centre of the town

1.) stocky _____

2.) rocky regions _____

3.) tree trunk _____

4.) stout _____

5.) slender _____

6.) downtown _____

7.) awesome _____

8.) inhabited _____

9.) sensational _____

10.) concoction _____

Answer these questions in complete sentences

1.) Why are the trees on Socatra Island called bottle trees?

_____

_____

2.) Where do they grow?

_____

_____

3.) What will you see if you travel to these rocky regions?

_____

_____

4.) What effect will those trees have on tourists?

_____

_____

What do these words and phrases from paragraphs 3 & 4 of the text mean? Choose from the following list.

ship / boat,   captures your attention,   something worth taking a photograph of,   a place where ships come when they are not at sea / a port,   the act of a ship coming into a harbour,   a village built on a mountain,   the bottom / the foot of something, really great,   a very busy harbour,   a very wide view, raised high,   the top

1.) photogenic _____

2.) mountain village _____

3.) marvelous _____

4.) captivating _____

5.) elevated _____

6.) peak _____

7.) base _____

8.) panoramic _____

9.) harbour _____

10.) bustling harbour _____

11.) vessel _____

12.)dock _____

Answer these questions in complete sentences

1.) Where can you find Al Qahira Fortress?

_____

_____

2.) Where is it situated?

_____

_____

3.) What will you discover if you stand at the base of the fort?

_____

_____

4.) What is the name of the key seaport of Yemen?

_____

_____

5.) What is this harbour mainly filled with?

_____

_____

6.) What will you find if you go there?

_____

_____

7.) What are there within the town?

_____

_____

Read the following passage. <u>Underline</u> the sentences that are in the first conditional and put a circle around the sentences that are in the future tense.

The front desk manager of a hotel is speaking to some of his staff. "If the bus-load of tourists comes after 6 o'clock, we will offer them dinner in the restaurant." One of the reception staff asked, "What if they come before 6 o'clock?" The manager answered, "If they come before 6 o'clock, we will give them tea and biscuits."

"Will they be happy with only tea and biscuits?" asked another of the reception staff. "Yes, I think they will be," responded the manager. "We will give them tea and biscuits before they go to their rooms. They will then be given their dinner later on in the afternoon or evening."

"When will they go sightseeing?" asked the tour guide operator. "They will be taken by bus to see the old city and surrounding areas tomorrow morning at 8am," said the manager. "If they finish the tour in the early afternoon, what will they do for the rest of the day?" asked one of the reception staff. "They will be given a tour of the museum and art gallery," said the manager.

UNIT 5
A job as a tour guide

Being a tour guide is great. You can travel while working and visit dream destinations all over the globe! You'll meet people from everywhere, wake up in a different city every other day, and truly become a world traveler. But do you know what it is really like and what it takes to get the job of a tour guide?

Being a tour guide doesn't mean you are on permanent vacation. It's a competitive field, and you'll have to work hard if you want to keep your job. You need to be dedicated, but you also need to know how to have fun. You'll live out of a suitcase, answer hundreds of questions every day, and work with many different personalities and cultures from all over the world. A tour guide is at the heart of a tour and how you deal with your travelers can make or break your career.

Your passengers have saved long and hard to come on your tour, and you need to do everything you can, every day, to make sure they have the trip of a lifetime. You need to be patient, fierce, tenacious, and most importantly possess a genuine passion for your passengers and profession.

You will really have to do your homework well if you want to be successful in your career as a tour guide. Your customers will ask you a lot of questions about the sites you take them to. So, the history and geography of these sites will have to be researched by you. If you want to remember all the details of these places, you will have to take notes and memorise them well.

Also, it will be necessary for you to find out what your customers want. Some travelers want hiking and walking holidays. If they do, you will have to be physically fit. You will also have learn the various routes to take them on.

Some travelers want to see historical sites. In this case, you will need to learn about the history of the places you take them to. Other travelers want to learn about the contemporary culture of a place. The tour guide then must know where art galleries, theatres and other cultural venues are located.

So a tour guide's job is interesting and rewarding, but it is not always easy. If you have your heart set on being a tour guide, you will have to prepare yourself for a lot of hard work.

What do these words and phrases from paragraphs 1 – 3 of the text mean? Choose from the following list.

persistent / not easily moved about,   real / true,   strong / aggressive,   a lot of people are doing (or wanting to do) the same job,   the centre of,   the world,   you are willing to wait,   all your belongings are in a suitcase,   a strong love for something,   every second day (Sunday – Tuesday – Thursday – Saturday –Monday .....),   a trip that will never be repeated and which is the best ever,   a type of person / his or her character, always on holiday,   a place you have always thought about traveling to,   devoted to something

1.) dream destinations _____

2.) globe _____

3.) every other day _____

4.) permanent vacation _____

5.) competitive field _____

6.) dedicated _____

7.) live out of a suitcase _____

_____

8.) personality _____

9.) heart of _____

10.) trip of a lifetime _____

11.) patient _____

12.) fierce _____

13.) tenacious_____

14.) passion _____

15.) genuine _____

Answer these questions in complete sentences

1.) Who will you meet if you become a tour guide?

_____

_____

2.) Apart from being dedicated, what do you need to do?

_____

_____

3.) What will you have to do if you want to keep your job?

_____

_____

4.) How many questions will you answer?

_____

_____

5.) What do you need to make sure your passengers have?

_____

_____

What do these words and phrases from paragraphs 4 - 6 of the text mean? Choose from the following list.

of the present day,   write in short form the important things of a text or of what someone has said,   to strongly desire something, to be able to remember and then recall something without looking

FRANCIS A. ANDREW

at a text or notes,   giving a lot of personal satisfaction,   a
way,   a place,   strong and energetic

1.) take notes _____

2.) memorise _____

3.) physically fit _____

4.) route _____

5.) contemporary _____

6.) venue _____

7.) rewarding _____

8.) heart set on _____

Answer these questions in complete sentences

1.) What will you have to do really well if you want to be a successful tour guide?

_____

_____

2.) What will have to be researched by you?

_____

_____

3.) What will be necessary for you to find out?

_____

_____

4.) What kind of travelers want to see theatres, art galleries and cultural venues?

_____

_____

5.) What will a prospective tour guide have to prepare himself for?

_____

_____

Complete the If Clauses 1 – 10 with the Main Clauses a - j

1.) If you don't want to get fat_____

_____

2.) If John wants to pass his exams_____

_____

3.) If Alan doesn't drive more carefully_____

_____

4.) If you knock on the door_____

_____

5.) If you improve your football-playing skills_____

_____

6.) If you look at a mobile phone for too long _____

_____

7.) If you smoke _____

_____

8.) If Tony doesn't hurry up _____

_____

9.) If Ali runs fast _____

_____

10.) If we ask the teacher _____

_____

a.) he will win the race

b.) you will have to stop eating so much

c.) he will be late

d.) he will need to study harder

e.) she will explain the difficult maths problem to us

f.) they will open it

g.) you will damage your lungs

h.) he will have an accident

i.) you will be able to play professionally

j.) you will seriously impair your vision

READING FOR ENJOYMENT
Dishes from Thailand

Tom Yum is a spicy Thai Soup with shrimp, and it is one of the most famous traditional foods in the country. It is typically made with mushroom, tomatoes, garlic, fish sauce, cilantro, onions, galangal, kaffir lime leaves, and lemongrass together with a lot of lime juice. Due to the composition of the ingredients, it is sour and spicy, but lovely to the taste buds. If it is served in a traditional way, the soup will have meats such as fish, beef, or chicken. It is generally served in a large clay bowl or an aluminum pot with a charcoal burner.

Laap has its origins in northeast Thailand, and it is one great dish you must never miss during your Thai visit. It is primarily made from minced meat seasoned with fresh herbs, fish sauce, lime juice, and roasted rice powder. The best way to enjoy this delicacy is to accompany it with sticky rice or fat grains of rice that have been steamed and eaten with hands.

If you have a liking for traditional foods that you can easily find in the streets, then you will have every reason to try out Phat Kaphrao. It is a traditional street food staple in Thailand, and it features a combination of meat flash-fried with basil. In most places, you will find it doused in a generous amount of chili and garlic. Mostly served over sticky rice and often topped with fried eggs – it is the definition of traditional Thai-style one-bite meal.

Khao soi is another famous traditional noodle dish that comes from the northern parts of the country. It is primarily a broth of soup that boasts of rich ingredients comprising of curry and coconut milk that gives it a rich, creamy consistency. It is common to find the broth topped over flat egg noodles that have further been topped up with deep fried egg noodles. Meats such as beef and chicken are also familiar accompaniments with khao soi. If you are a lover of soup, you will have to try this dish.

If there is one traditional Thai food known across the globe, then it will be Pad Thai. It is a stir-fried rice noodle cooked in a very hot wok with chili, garlic, tofu and eggs amongst other ingredients. Some of the popular meats you are likely to encounter in Pad Thai include shrimp and chicken, and don't be surprised if you find it garnished with lime juice, peanuts, spring onions and sprouts. It is a one hearty and comforting Thai meal you will be glad to not to have missed.

The Thai green curry with chicken is another incredibly popular dish in Thailand and one you should try if you want to understand more about the roots of Thai foods. If you enjoy curries, you will love this one. This curry is comprised of coconut milk, green curry paste, and chicken as the main ingredients, though you could always replace the chicken with any meat of your choice. The green curry paste comes from a blend of shallots, garlic, and green chilies amongst other ingredients. The coconut milk is where the soup gets the rich, creamy consistency, while the green curry paste makes it hot and sweet. It is best enjoyed with a plate of rice.

Answer the questions in complete sentences

1.) Why is Tom Yum sour and spicy?

_____

_____

2.) How is it served?

_____

_____

3.) If it is served in a traditional way, what meats will it have?

_____

_____

4.) What is Laap primarily made of?

_____

_____

5.) What kind of rice is best to eat with Laap?

_____

_____

6.) If you have a liking for traditional Thai street foods, what dish will you try out?

_____

_____

7.) If you are a lover of soup, which dish will you have to try?

_____

_____

8.) If there is one traditional food that is known everywhere in the world, what will it be?

_____

_____

9.) If someone enjoys curries, which one will they try?

_____

_____

10.) What is it comprised of?

_____

_____

THEME 20

TRANSPORTATION IN OMAN AND THE GULF

UNIT 1
Transport Abu Dhabi

Revision: Conditional Type 2 sentence

Basheer and Abdullah are imagining what they would do if things were different in their lives.

B: If I got a million dollars, I would buy a big house.

A: If I had a lot of money, I would go on a world cruise.

B: What would you do if you achieved 100% in all your exams?

A: I would go to Harvard University in America.

B: If I went to Harvard University, I would study Physics.

A: I would study Engineering.

B: Where would you go if you had a free airline ticket?

A: If I had a free airline ticket, I would fly to Paris.

B: If I became a professional footballer, I would play for the Omani national team.

A: If I could invent something, I would design a flying car.

Answer the questions in complete sentences

1.) What would Basheer do if he got a million dollars?

_____

_____

2.) Where would Abdullah go if he had a lot of money?

_____

_____

3.) Which university would Abdullah go to if he got full marks in his examinations?

_____

_____

4.) Which subjects would Basheer and Abdullah study if they went to this university?

_____

_____

5.) Where would Abdullah travel to if he had a free airline ticket?

_____

_____

6.) Who would Basheer play for if he became a professional football player?

_____

_____

7.) If Abdullah could invent something, what would he invent?

_____

_____

Complete these sentences using the second conditional

Example: I drove through red / police catch

If I drove through a red light, the police would catch me.

1.) you ate a box of chocolates every day / get very fat

_____

_____

2.) he acted in films / be famous

_____

_____

3.) Susan owned a company / be very rich

_____

_____

4.) John lived in Australia / see kangaroos

_____

_____

5.) lived in Germany / speak German fluently

_____

_____

Read this information about *Transport Abu Dhabi*

We have had a lot of experience in the taxi business. We have been caring for our passengers for many years. We have taken the initiative to make their journeys to their homes/hotels as smooth as possible. Our luxury airport taxis with professional drivers have been driving passengers arriving at Abu Dhabi International Airport around-the-clock since 1977.

Regardless of which terminal you are arriving at, you will find a reliable, 24-hour metered taxi service ready to transport you to your final destination. See below to find out about the particular services you can look forward to at the respective terminals. We have had a lot of success in this business, and we have been improving our service on a regular basis.

If you are arriving at Terminals 1 or 3

You will find us at the clearly signposted taxi pick-up area at the lower curbside outside Arrivals Hall for Terminals 1 & 3. Here, you will easily spot our fleet of 6-seater black Mercedes Vitos.

With these luxury taxis, you will enjoy:

- Extra baggage space
- Plush interiors
- Multi-lingual male and female drivers with an excellent knowledge of Abu Dhabi and the UAE (also equipped with up-to-date GPS systems)
- Acceptance of multiple currencies

We have arranged vehicles for people with special needs and for the elderly.

If you are arriving at Terminal 2

Metered Toyota Camry taxis are available outside the Terminal 2 Arrivals area. We have made some maps to show you exactly where you can find us.

Fares

Meter Starting Fare (Flag Fall) – AED 25.00

Every 1 km up to 50 km (6am-10pm) – AED 1.6

Every 1 km up to 50 kms (10pm – 6am) – AED 1.69

Every 1 km over 50 kms – 9 fils extra

Every 1 minute of waiting time (first 5 minutes free) – 50 fils

As a holder of a discount card from the UAE Ministry of Social Affairs, you will receive a reduction of 25% to 50% on your taxi fare.

Contact information

If you need any further help regarding your taxi service, you will be able to call the Transport Abu Dhabi Call Centre on 600 535353.

If you would prefer a private limousine, enquire at any of our Customer Service desks and one will be arranged for you.

What do these words and phrases from the text mean? Choose from the following list.

24 hours,   dependable / you can be sure of something,   look after,   a notice showing you where something is located,   to be the first to do something,   particular,   abundance / ease / comfort,   make something better,   a part of the airport where planes start and finish their journeys,   a taxi with a device to show the passengers the prices,   despite / no matter what

1.) care for _____

2.) initiative _____

3.) luxury _____

4.) around-the-clock _____

5.) regardless _____

6.) terminal _____

7.) reliable _____

8.) metred taxi _____

9.) respective _____

10.) improve _____

11.) signposted _____

Answer these questions in complete sentences

1.) What have Transport Abu Dhabi had a lot of experience in?

_____

_____

2.) What has this company been doing for many years?

_____

_____

3.) What have they taken the initiative n?

_____

_____

4.) What have their luxury airport taxis been doing since 1977?

_____

_____

5.) What has this company had a lot of success in?

_____

_____

6.) What have they been doing on a regular basis?

_____

_____

What do these words and phrases from the text mean? Choose from the following list.

to provide equipment and materials for a particular action,   a special permit that gives the holder a reduced price,   things that usually disabled people require,   the end part of a pavement where it borders the street,   to ask for information,   posh / luxurious,   older people,   to organise,   places to store your suitcases and other luggage,   the part of the airport where passengers go to when they have finished their journey

1.) curbside _____

2.) Arrivals Hall _____

3.) baggage space _____

4.) plush _____

5.) equipped _____

6.) elderly _____

7.) special needs _____

8.) discount card _____

9.) enquire _____

10.) arranged _____

Answer these questions in complete sentences

1.) Where will you find the company clearly signposted?

_____

_____

2.) Who has the company arranged vehicles for?

_____

_____

3.) What has the company made?

_____

_____

4.) How much is the metre starting fare?

_____

_____

5.) What will you be able to do if you need further help?

_____

_____

6.) What would I have to do if I preferred a private limousine?

_____

_____

UNIT 2
Buses from Muscat to Dubai

The Road Transport Authority (RTA) has launched a bus service between Muscat and Dubai. Here are some of the main features of this service:

- One way journey lasts six hours and costs Dh55, while the return ticket costs just Dh90
- The three daily buses will start at 7.30am, 3.30pm and 11pm.
- Passengers can embark from three stops: Abu Hail Metro Station, Dubai Airport Terminal 2 and Rashidiya Metro Station

Dubai: You can now hop on to an RTA bus for a trip to Muscat for as little as Dh55.

On Monday, the RTA in partnership with Mwasalat, Oman's national transport company, have launched three daily trips to Muscat.

The one way journey lasts six hours. A single ticket costs Dh55, while the return ticket costs just Dh90.

Passengers can embark on the trip from three locations in Dubai, starting from, Abu Hail Metro Station, Dubai Airport Terminal 2 and Rashidiya Metro Station.

The three daily buses will start at 7.30am, 3.30pm and 11pm.

In Oman the buses will have eleven stops on the way to Muscat including Shinas, Sohar, Barka, Muscat Airport and Athiba Bus Stations in Muscat. The buses will stop at these stops on the way back as well.

With a capacity of 50 passengers, the luxury buses have been installed with the latest tech features including free WiFi, adaptive cruise control and drive assist for additional safety. Passengers have been enjoying these facilities since the Muscat to Dubai service started.

Tickets can initially be bought only over the counter and in the next stage online ticketing system and nol payment will also be available.

The Dubai-Muscat bus service by Oman's Mwasalat has been running for several years with three daily buses.

However, Ahmad Behroozian, CEO of RTA's Public Transport Agency said the new joint offering will add value to existing services with new buses and more stops.

He added that the location of the stops were carefully chosen and will particularly help passengers, offering greater rail, land and air connectivity.

Several private transport operators have also been running daily buses between Dubai and Oman.

What do these words and phrases from the text mean? Choose from the following list.

Chief Executive Officer – the top man or woman in a company, a ticket which takes you to one destination where you finish your journey,   a system where two companies work together on a business project,   offered by two companies,   get on a vehicle, a ticket which allows you to return to where you originally began your journey,   fit something into a place,   quickly get on a vehicle,   to buy the ticket at the office / without buying it in advance

1.) single ticket _____

2.) return ticket _____

3.) embark _____

4.) hop on _____

5.) partnership _____

6.) install _____

7.) over the counter _____

8.) CEO _____

9.) joint offering _____

Answer these questions in complete sentences

1.) What does RTA stand for?

_____

_____

2.) What has the RTA done?

_____

_____

3.) How long does the journey take between the two destinations?

_____

_____

4.) How much do the two types of ticket cost?

_____

_____

5.) How many stops will the buses have in Oman?

_____

_____

6.) What is the passenger capacity of the buses?

_____

_____

7.) How long have passengers been enjoying the facilities provided by the buses?

_____

_____

8.) How long has the Dubai to Muscat bus service been running?

_____

_____

9.) Who is Ahmad Behroozian?

_____

_____

10.) What have several private transport operators been doing?

_____

_____

Ali and Saleh are having a conversation. This is the first time they have met for a few years

A: Where are you living now, Saleh?

S: I am living in Bidbid.

A: How long have you been living in Bidbid?

S: I have been living there since 2015.

FRANCIS A. ANDREW

A: Where are you working now?

S: I have opened my own business. It is a car showroom. I have been running it for two years. What have you been doing since I last saw you, Ali?

A: I am still living in Nizwa. I have lived there all my life, so I want to stay there.

S: What about your job? Have you got a job, Ali?

A: I have started my own furniture shop? I have been selling furniture for three years.

S: Have you been doing business locally?

A: I was selling locally for two years. I have been selling furniture nationally since last year. I will start exporting to other Gulf countries later on this year.

Answer the following questions in complete sentences

1.) Where is Saleh living now?

_____

_____

2.) How long has he been living there?

_____

_____

3.) How long has he been running the car showroom?

_____

_____

4.) How long has Ali lived in Nizwa?

_____

_____

5.) How long has he been selling furniture?

_____

_____

6.) How long was he selling locally for?

_____

_____

7.) How long has he been selling furniture nationally for?

_____

_____

8.) When will he start exporting to other Gulf countries?

_____

_____

UNIT 3
Traffic congestion in Dubai

Road congestions remain a problem for residents in Dubai, where drivers in the emirate have spent an average of 80 hours stuck in traffic jams. These statistics were for the year 2018, and were compiled by a research team.

The report, has just been released by traffic information supplier Inrix They have shown that Dubai is the most congested city in the UAE and 79th in the world.

In Abu Dhabi, drivers spent an average of 50 hours sitting in their cars during peak traffic in 2018, making the UAE capital one of the least congested urban areas in the world -- ranked 180th out of more than 200 cities.

Traffic congestions in Dubai are worse than in Vancouver, Cape Town, Copenhagen, Manchester or Austin.

The good news is that the level of gridlock experienced by Dubai drivers isn't as bad as in many other commercial centres in other countries.

In terms of the amount of time lost due to congestion, residents in Bogota had it worst, with the average driver spending 272 hours sitting behind the wheel during traffic jams last year, followed by Rome (254 hours) and Dublin (246 hours).

In the United States, drivers lost 97 hours a year due to congestion, costing them nearly $87 billion in 2018 or an average of $1,348 per driver.

The Inrix 2018 Global Traffic Scorecard is an annual study of traffic congestions in more than 200 cities worldwide. In the 2017 study, analysts looked at the time spent in congestion for the average commuter.

Overall, Moscow has been ranked by Inrix as the most congested city in the world. Istanbul has come second, followed by Bogota, Mexico City and Sao Paulo in the top five. Inrex has been analyzing congestion in cities for nearly ten years.

What do these words and phrases from the text mean? Choose from the following list.

level,   to collect slowly and then publish,   traffic jam in which a grid of intersecting streets is so completely congested that no vehicular movement is possible,   to study something / check,   a single value that summarises or represents the general significance of a set of unequal values,   someone who travels to and from work over a long distance on a daily basis,   numerical information

1.) statistics _____

2.) compile _____

3.) average _____

4.) rank _____

5.) gridlock _____

6.) commuter _____

7.) analyse _____

Answer the following questions in complete sentences

1.) On average, how many hours have motorists in Dubai spent stuck in traffic jams?

_____

_____

2.) For what years were these statistics?

_____

_____

3.) Who has just released this report?

_____

_____

4.) What have they shown?

_____

_____

5.) What is the good news?

_____

_____

6.) How many hours did drivers lose to congestion in the United States?

_____

_____

7.) What is The Inrix 2018 Global Traffic Scorecard?

_____

_____

8.) What did analysts do in 2017?

_____

_____

9.) Which city did Inrix rank as the most congested one in the world?

_____

_____

10.) Which city has come second?

_____

_____

11.) What has Inrex been doing for ten years?

_____

_____

Change these past simple tense sentences into the present perfect tense

Example: I ate a sandwich.

I have eaten a sandwich

1.) I drank some tea.

_____

2.) Mother cooked a meal.

_____

3.) Father repaired the car.

_____

4.) We did our homework.

_____

5.) They gave sweets to the children.

_____

6.) Ben swam in the sea.

_____

Change these past simple tense sentences into the present perfect continuous tense

Example: I made some coffee.

I have been making some coffee.

1.) Bob and his friends played football.

_____

2.) She watched a programme on TV.

_____

3.) The teacher taught a lesson.

_____

4.) The pupils listened to the lesson.

_____

5.) Mr. Smith drove to London.

_____

6.) The birds flew in the sky.

_____

_____

UNIT 4
Oman Airports

Revision: conditional type 3 sentences

Tareq and Raed are talking about some things that went wrong yesterday.

T: If I had known you were coming, I would have met you at the airport. I am so sorry.

R: That's OK. You didn't know I was coming so you didn't meet me at the airport. If my mobile phone had had some credit in it, I would have phoned you.

T: If you hadn't missed the last bus, you would not have had to stay in a hotel.

R: If I had found a taxi, I would have gone straight to your house.

T: If Omar had come to the office earlier, you would have caught an earlier flight.

R: I couldn't get you the chocolates at the Duty Free. If I hadn't arrived so late, I would have bought you the chocolates which you had asked for.

T: How is Ahmed.

R: He is OK. If he hadn't driven so recklessly, he wouldn't have caused an accident.

T: If he hadn't caused an accident, he wouldn't be in hospital now.

Answer the questions in complete sentences

1.) What would Tareq have done if he had known Raed was coming?

_____

_____

2.) What would Raed have done if his mobile phone had had some credit in it?

_____

_____

3.) What would Raed not have had to do if he hadn't missed the last bus?

_____

_____

4.) What would Raed have done if he had found a taxi?

_____

_____

5.) What would Raed have done if Omar had come to the office earlier?

_____

_____

6.) What didn't Raed do at the Duty Free?

_____

_____

7.) What would he have bought at the Duty Free if he hadn't arrived so late?

_____

_____

8.) Whom would he have bought them for?

_____

_____

9.) What wouldn't have happened if Ahmed had driven more carefully?

_____

_____

10.) Where would Ahmed not be now if he hadn't caused an accident?

_____

_____

Read about *Oman Airports*

Oman Airports is a government-owned company that manages and operates the civil airports in the Sultanate of Oman and provides integrated airport operations and infrastructure management, such as on-ground services, terminal buildings, cargo buildings, runways, aprons, car parking and other facilities.

- Manage the airport assets, facilities, infrastructure, projects and maintenance plans.
- Manage the Aerodrome Certification & Compliance, Emergency Planning, Capacity Management and Customer Services.
- Ensure operational readiness of new airports to support smooth opening of new airports and efficiency of key operational processes.
- Undertake airfield, terminal, flight information and firefighting systems management.
- Manage all the airport facilities and commercial areas such as retail, real estate, fuel farm, concession agreements, car park, airport space advertising, corporate communications and airline marketing.
- Carry out the Information, Communications and Technology management at the airports.

- Undertake financial services management and revenue collection from aeronautical and non-aeronautical sources and expenditure payments.
- Develop procurement policies and procedures.
- Provide and develop human resources and administration support for the corporate needs
- Facilitate and manage security
- Undertake Health, Safety and Environmental Management for all organizations operating within the airport boundaries.

The total staff strength at Oman Airports is more than 1200 employees with an Omanization level of approximately 94%.

Our vision is to be among the top world 20 airports.

Our purpose is constructing gateways to beauty and opportunities.

Our mission is to ensure that together, we can excellently manage and develop the gateways of Oman.

What do these words and phrases from the text mean? Choose from the following list.

the extensive paved part of an airport immediately adjacent to the terminal area or hangars,   the entire property of a person or company,   a plan to get something done,   connected / interlinked,   a system of public works and communications system of a country,   airfield / airport,   to agree to perform a task,   the goods or merchandise conveyed in a ship,   airplane, or vehicle / freight,   management system approved and shown to be operating to certain standards,   services on the ground at an airport

1.) integrated _____

2.) infrastructure _____

3.) ground services _____

4.) cargo _____

5.) apron _____

6.) assets _____

7.) project _____

8.) Certification and Compliance _____

9.) undertake _____

Answer these questions in complete sentences

1.) Is Oman Airports privately owned or government owned?

_____

_____

2.) What does it manage?

_____

_____

3.) What does it provide?

_____

_____

4.) What does it ensure?

_____

_____

5.) What does it undertake?

_____

_____

What do these words and phrases from the text mean? Choose from the following list.

a border / a mark between one thing or place and another,   a system whereby Omani people do jobs currently done by expatriates,   selling directly to the public without intermediaries,   properties in buildings and land,   income, a special privilege,   buying and selling in a market, obtaining supplies of a certain product,   an association / a company

1.) retail _____

2.) real estate _____

3.) corporate _____

4.) marketing _____

5.) revenue _____

6.) procurement _____

7.) boundary _____

8.) Omanisation _____

Answer these questions in complete sentences

1.) What does Oman Airports carry out?

_____

_____

2.) What does it develop?

_____

_____

3.) What does it facilitate?

_____

_____

4.) What is their vision?

_____

_____

5.) What is their mission?

_____

_____

6.) What is their purpose?

_____

_____

Use either *for* or *since* to complete these sentences

1.) My brother has been living in Salalah _____ three years.

2.) I have worked for the pdo _____ 2002.

3.) My friend has been at college _____ last year

4.) My sister has been cooking the dinner _____ an hour

5.) The boys have been playing football _____ three o'clock.

6.) The class has been working on the project _____ Tuesday.

7.) The construction workers have been building that house _____eight months.

8.) The artist has been painting that picture _____ January.

9.) Bill and John have had that car _____they were married.

10.) You have been working in that company _____ several weeks.

UNIT 5
Traveling around Oman

National Ferries Company (NFC)

Our Mission has always been to connect people by providing unique ferry operations that puts customer service experience at the forefront. As a team we have been aiming to create value for our stakeholders by maintaining the highest maritime standards. Our unified vision has been and always will be a renowned world class National Carrier for maritime ferry service of people's choice contributing to Oman's sustainable development.

Oman National Transport Company (MWASALAT)

The company has been in existence since 1972. It has been a permanent member of the International Association of Public Transport (UITP) since 1983, and is the leading public transport company in the Sultanate of Oman

In July 1984, the MWASALAT was awarded, by Royal Decree, the concession for providing the public transport services to all parts of the Sultanate of Oman. Since then, Mwasalat has been steadily advancing in the transport sector

In November 2015, the company launched its new identity "MWASALAT ". It is taking great strides in the development of public transport in the Sultanate .MWASALAT offers a number of services including: transportation within city and intercity, transport to schools, universities and transportation for special events. It has also undertaken t private transport contracts.

Other means of transport

Taxis and cabs are available in different parts of the Sultanate. These cars can even be used to reach various governorates and regions in Oman. There are quite a few of these companies, such as Alo Oman: www.clevertaxi.com.

Other semi-public transport services have been running in a number of regions, such as the minibus service.

Car Rental

Many car hire companies have been operating throughout the Sultanate since the 1970's. Some of these are franchise branches while others are local companies.

Salam Air

Salam Air is Oman's very first Low-Cost Carrier which aims to open the skies for everyone.

Its goal is to give people choice and flexibility when shaping their journeys and offer great experiences. Salam Air want to make air travel more affordable so more people can fly more often. They have always wanted to allow everyone to explore new destinations, expand their horizons and connect with their family & friends, whilst never compromising on quality and simplicity.

For more information and booking visit Salam Air website at https://salamair.com/

What do these words and phrases from the text mean? Choose from the following list.

an order given by a king or a queen, an area under a governing authority, achieving human needs and goals while protecting the natural environment, one of a kind / nothing else like it, not too fast and not too slow, the right or license granted to an individual or group to market a company's goods or services in a particular territory, half, a boat for a short sea trip, a small part of a larger company usually located in another part of the country, an individual or organization engaged in transporting passengers or goods for hire, between cities, a long step, connected to the sea, someone who has an interest in a business, the distinguishing character or personality of an individual, to give someone or an organization something for doing something great

1.) unique _____

2.) ferry _____

3.) stakeholder _____

4.) maritime _____

5.) carrier _____

6.) sustainable development _____

7.) award _____

8.) Royal Decree _____

9.) steadily _____

10.) identity _____

11.) stride _____

12.) intercity _____

13.) governate _____

14.) franchise _____

15.) branch _____

Answer these questions in complete sentences

1.) What do the letters NFC stand for?

_____

_____

2.) What has NFC's mission always been?

_____

_____

3.) What have they been aiming to create for their stakeholders?

_____

_____

4.) What can you say about their unified vision?

_____

_____

5.) What is another name for MWASALAT?

_____

_____

6.) How long has it been in existence?

_____

_____

7.) How long has it been a permanent member of the International Association of Public Transport?

_____

_____

8.) What has MWASALAT been doing since July 1984?

_____

_____

9.) What has the company undertaken?

_____

_____

What do these words and phrases from the text mean? Choose from the following list.

increase your range of knowledge, can be changed and adapted easily, not hard / not difficult / easy to understand, it is not to expensive, an agreement where no one gets everything

1.) flexibility _____

2.) affordable _____

3.) expand your horizons _____

4.) compromise _____

5.) simplicity _____

Answer these questions in complete sentences

1.) Where have other semi-transport services been running?

_____

_____

2.) What has been operating throughout the Sultanate since the 1970's?

_____

_____

3.) What have Salam Air always wanted?

_____

_____

4.) Where can you get more information on Salam Air?

_____

_____

Make present perfect sentences with these words.

Examples: Bill / live Muscat / eleven years

Bill has lived in Muscat for eleven years

Bob and Benny / work in that company / 2002

Bob and Benny have worked in that company since 2002

1.) That shop / sell newspapers / five months

_____

_____

2.) The teacher / teach Maths / 2012

_____

_____

3.) The children / eat their dinner

_____

_____

4.) Bobby /do his homework

_____

_____

5.) We / make some tea

_____

_____

Make present perfect continuous sentences with these words

Examples: Ahmed / drive Muscat /8 o'clock this morning

Ahmed has been driving to Muscat since 8 o'clock this morning.

The managers/ talk / two hours

The managers have been talking for two hours

1.) Thomas / read / an hour

_____

_____

2.) The students / study / two hours

_____

_____

3.) I /drink tea / five minutes

_____

_____

4.) You / teach / 10 o'clock

_____

_____

5.) The mechanic / repair the car / this afternoon

_____

_____

READING FOR ENJOYMENT

The Arab world is known for its wide deserts, especially the Rub' Al Khali (the Empty Quarter), with its golden sands. Here is everything you need to know about the famous Rub' Al Khali Desert for your next visit to Oman.

What is the Empty Quarter?

The Empty Quarter is the English name for the Rub' Al Khali desert, located in the southern part of the Arabian Peninsula. It is the largest continuous sand sea in the world, with an area of 650,000 square kilometres (250,000 sq mi), and 1,000 kilometres (620 mi) long and 500 kilometres (310 mi) wide. The Al Rub' Al Khali desert is shared by four countries: Saudi Arabia, Yemen, the United Arab Emirates and Oman.

The surface of the desert is covered by reddish-orange colored sand dunes, which reach around 250 metres (820 ft) high, and several lake beds. It is believed that the lake beds were originally shallow lakes formed by monsoon rains thousands of years ago, and only lasted for a few years.

Al Rub' Al Khali, as one of the most significant sand seas in the world, has been featured in several international films, such as *Star Wars: The Force Awakens, The Matrix, The Panther* and many others.

The Empty Quarter Sand Dunes © Nepenthes Wikipedia Commons

How to get to the Empty Quarter

The Empty Quarter is located in the Governorate of Dhofar in southern Oman, so it is better to fly to Oman through Salalah International Airport. Tourists can also fly to Muscat International Airport, but from there will need either to fly or drive to Salalah by car or bus.

Several companies provide tours and guides to visit the magnificent sandy desert, such as Al Fawaz Tours, Safaridrive.com, Original Travel, Light Foot Travel, and Oman Day Tours. Tours include one-day trips through the desert with a skilled Bedouin guide, 4×4 driving and camping under the bright stars.

Activities in the Empty Quarter

Visitors can enjoy a 4×4 drive in the desert or a camel ride, or camp out on the dunes. One of the best experiences in the Empty Quarter is to spend some time with the Bedouins of the desert. Visitors can enjoy listening to old stories about Oman, its culture and the desert. They will be introduced to the lifestyle, homes, and food of the Bedouin people.

Best places to stay and eat in the Empty Quarter

Due to the harsh environment of the Empty Quarter, there are no touristy places or facilities such as hotels. However, tourists are encouraged to spend a night or two camping on the stunning dunes, under the clear sky and the bright stars of Dhofar. Tour companies have camps with tents.

As for food, most companies have local Bedouins cook traditional Omani food for visitors. Other companies prepare their own food.

Weather in the Empty Quarter

The region is classified as "hyper-arid", which means that it lacks water for the growth of plants or survival of animals. Rainfall is less than 3 cm (1.2 in) every year. The daily temperatures are between 47 °C (117 °F) and 51 °C (124 °F).

Empty Quarter Desert © Land Rover MENA Flickr

The people of the Empty Quarter

Despite the severe environment of the Al Rub' Al Khali desert, several tribes from the Arabian Peninsula have managed to establish life on its sands. Most tribes that live there do so close to the edge of the desert. Few roads exist to help settlers find water spots and oil production centers.

Desert Safari © Robert Haandrikman Flickr

Tips to follow before you visit the Empty Quarter

Bring light clothes, big hats, high-quality sunglasses and a jacket and sweater for the cold nights. Due to the conservative nature of Omani culture and the Bedouins, don't bring short clothes or swimwear that is very revealing.

Answer the following questions in complete sentences

1.) Where is the Empty Quarter located?

_____

_____

2.) How many countries share the Rub' Al Khali desert? Name
    them.

_____

_____

3.) How high are the sand dunes?

_____

_____

4.) Which films has the Rub' Al Khali been featured in?

_____

_____

5.) What will visitors to the Empty Quarter be introduced to?

_____

_____

6.) Why are there no 'touristy places' in the Empty Quarter?

_____

_____

7.) Why is the region classed as 'hyper-arid?'

_____

_____

8.) How much rainfall does the region get per annum?

_____

_____

9.) Where do most of the tribes of the Empty Quarter live?

_____

_____

10.) Why do you need a jacket and a sweater if you go to the Empty Quarter?

_____

_____

THEME 21

NEWS AND THE MEDIA

UNIT 1
Television Cameramen

Cameramen or camerawomen record moving images for film, television, commercials, music videos or for corporate productions. They operate film or digital video cameras. They do this under the supervision of the director or director of photography. Here are the things the cameramen do.

They set up and put into position, the camera equipment. They choose the correct lenses and camera angles. They plan shots. They rehearse the shots. They follow a camera shooting plan and take cues from the director. If they are in a studio, they will also take instructions from the floor manager. They have to deal with various technical issues. Also, they have to co-operate with other technical departments dealing with sound and lighting.

Sometimes there is only one cameraman. When so, the cameraman uses a single portable camera. At other times there is an entire camera crew. This is generally the case when producing feature films and drama productions. There are certain jobs for certain cameramen in these types of production.

The first assistant camera (also known as the focus puller) judges and adjusts the focus on each shot.

The second assistant camera (also known as the clapper loader) has the duties of loading and unloading film, counting the number of shot takes, and generally assisting the camera crew.

Then there is the grip. This involves building and operating cranes and pulleys needed to move a camera during shooting.

Generally, cameramen specialise in either film or television work, as the equipment and techniques can be different. However, with the advances in digital cameras and HD technology, it is becoming more common for cameramen to work in both jobs.

What do these words and phrases from the paragraph mean? Choose from the following list.

to become an expert in something,   repeat something many times so as to improve upon the performance of it,   to make the camera lens produce a clear picture,   advertisements for company products,   a team of people working together,   usual / the norm,   to make some changes,   helping,   you can carry it around,   concerned with companies,   when to do something,   work with,   taking film out of the camera, direction and instructions,   improvement,   the situation / the circumstances,   put into position,   putting film into the camera,   to say what is right or wrong,   the eye of the camera, a segment of motion recorded by the camera,   the boss in a filming studio,   a way or method of doing something

1.) commercials _____

2.) corporate _____

3.) supervision _____

4.) set up _____

5.) director _____

6.) lens _____

7.) rehearse _____

8.) cue _____

9.) co-operate _____

10.) portable _____

11.) crew _____

12.) the case _____

13.) judge _____

14.) adjust _____

15.) focus _____

16.) shot _____

17.) loading film _____

18.) unloading film _____

19.) assisting _____

20.) specialise _____

21.) technique _____

22.) advances _____

23.) common _____

Answer these questions in complete sentences.

1.) What are the two kinds of camera mentioned in the text?

_____

_____

2.) What do cameramen and camera women do with the camera equipment?

_____

_____

3.) Who do the camera people take cues from?

_____

_____

4.) Where will they take instructions from the floor manager?

_____

_____

5.) Which departments will the camera people have to co-operate with?

_____

_____

6.) When is a portable camera used?

_____

_____

7.) What does the first cameraman do?

_____

_____

8.) Who has the duties of loading and unloading film?

_____

_____

9.) Why does the grip build and operate cranes and pulleys?

_____

_____

10.) What is making it possible for camera people to work in both film and television work?

_____

_____

Say if these sentences are true (T) or false (F)

1.) The second assistant has the job of counting the number of shot takes. _____

2.) The director or the director of photography work under the supervision of the cameramen. _____

3.) Cameramen and women choose the wrong lenses and camera angles. _____

4.) They follow a camera shooting plan. _____

5.) Camera crews film drama scenes and feature films. _____

6.) The first assistant is also known as the clapper loader. _____

Choose *a*, *b*, *c* or *d*

1.) Camera operators record _____

a.) still images   b.) moving images   c.) directors   d.) angles

2.) Camera people plan _____

a.) feature films   b.) lenses   c.) television   d.) shots

3.) They have to deal with technical _____.

a.) issues   b.) cameras   c.) lighting   d.) sound

4.) _____ kinds of camera people are listed in the text.

a.) One   b.) Two   c.) Three   d.) Four

5.) The _____ assists the camera crew.

a.) first assistant   b.) second assistant   c.) the grip   d.) the fourth assistant

6.) Generally, camera people _____ in television or film work.

a.) specialises   b.) specialisation   c.) to specialise
d.) specialise

UNIT 2
Choosing a career

The career you choose is one of the most important decisions of your life. The right career brings you success and happiness. But if you make a wrong choice, through using information that is too simple or not properly researched, it can damage your prospects, relationships and prosperity for the rest of your life. Here is some advice for you to follow when you are making a career choice.

You might want to consider factors such as the type of lifestyle you want and the ethics of the company you intend to be employed by.

Your choice of career may be limited by financial or geographical considerations, family responsibilities, physical disability or your qualifications.

You might want to think about whether or not you would like to have a family and settle down. Ask yourself if you want just one job for the rest of your life or would like to have the option to change career. Would you be interested in setting up your own business? Do you want to retire early or late in life?

It is important to find out if your chosen career gives you many opportunities in life. You can find opportunities by responding to advertisements for jobs or by engaging in vocational training. Then there is networking through people you know to get referrals to potential employers.

Your personality is very important. It is important to have a positive and gregarious personality when you are choosing a career path because employers like employees to have this kind of personality.

What do these words and phrases from the text mean? Choose from the following list.

a choice, a way along which your career will develop, the type of job you will do for most of your life, academic certificates you get after studying at an educational institution, contacting people on the internet, enjoying being with other people, taking part in something, to send someone somewhere – usually for advice, the chances and opportunities you have in your life, your character / the type of person you are, a condition existing between two or more people, give up working – usually due to advanced age, opposite of negative / being optimistic, the kind of life you lead, morals / good behaviour, wealth, some kind of damage to your body that impairs your movements in some way, answering, something to think about / to ponder over, stop traveling and stay in one place, a possible future employer, something you have to do

1.) career _____

2.) prospects _____

3.) prosperity _____

4.) relationship _____

5.) lifestyle _____

6.) ethics _____

7.) responsibility _____

8.) consideration _____

9.) physical disability _____

10.) qualifications _____

11.) settle down _____

12.) option _____

13.) retire _____

14.) responding _____

15.) engaging _____

16.) referral _____

17.) potential employer _____

18.) networking _____

19.) personality _____

20.) positive _____

21.) gregarious _____

22.) career path _____

Answer these questions in complete sentences.

1.) What is the most important decision of your life?

_____

_____

2.) What two factors does the text suggest you might want to consider?

_____

_____

3.) What may limit your choice of career?

_____

_____

4.) What question might you ask yourself?

_____

_____

5.) What might you be interested in setting up?

_____

_____

6.) What should your chosen career give you?

_____

_____

7.) How can you find opportunities?

_____

_____

8.) With whom do you do networking?

_____

_____

9.) To whom do you get referrals?

_____

_____

10.) Why is it important to have a positive and gregarious personality?

_____

_____

Say if these sentences are true (T) or false (F)

1.) The kind of career you choose is unimportant. _____

2.) If you choose the proper career, you will be successful and happy. _____

3.) Choosing the wrong career can be damaging for many aspects of your life. _____

4.) Settling down and having a family is not something you should think about. _____

5.) Vocational training is not a serious consideration. _____

6.) Employers like their employees to have outgoing personalities. _____

Choose *a*, *b*, *c* or *d*.

1.) A synonym for *might* is _____

a.) think   b.) consider   c.) career   d.) may

2.) Wrong choices can be made through information that is too _____.

    a.) simple   b.) hard   c.) good   d.) sophisticated

3.) Bad _____ can damage your life.

    a.) choose   b.) chose   c.) choices   d.) choice

4.) You might want to set up your own _____.

    a.) referral   b.) business   c.) choice   d.) damage

5.) Having a positive personality is _____.

    a.) unimportant   b.) important   c.) wrong   d.) bad

UNIT 3
How newspaper reporters get their stories.

Journalists obtain their information from a number of sources that help them in writing up their stories and news items. In some cases, their information comes from personal contacts, but mostly they hail from public sources.

The first of these public sources is called a news agency. A news agency is either a public or private organization that gathers, writes and distributes news from around the country and the world. The three most notable news agencies are Reuters News, Associated Press(AP) and Agence France- Press (AFP).

It is important for journalists to be familiar with a large number of news sources. It is essential that they subscribe to and read the following: newspapers, online outlets, magazines, the television news, the radio news, newsletters, Twitter lists, podcasts, forums, comment sections, reddits, and blogs.

Some companies use what are called press releases (PR) when they want to promote a product or provide information and themselves.

Events are important sources of information for journalists. Conferences, festivals and trade fairs provide journalists with a wealth of information. For example, many science and technology journalists will attend a science fair to see the newest IT innovations.

Social media is used by a large number of journalists. Twitter is what is most accessed by journalists.

What do these words and phrases from the text mean? Choose from the following list.

a piece of news,   bring together things from various places into one place,   a gathering of a large number of people to speak on a particular subject or issue,   to be able to get into something,   a celebration of entertaining events,   someone whose job it is to collect information to write up as a news story / sometimes they are called reporters,   a website that contains personal information,   something worthy of consideration,   a large gathering in which various companies in a particular field or industry show their products to potential customers,   a platform, extremely important,   to tell the public how important a product is / advertising a product,   people whom you know,   come from,   opposite of gather / to move from a central place and put in different places,   a network of communal interests,   to know someone or something well / not the first time to see this, an invention,   a place where something begins / has its origins, to give your name to something

1.) journalist _____

2.) source _____

3.) news item _____

4.) personal contacts _____

5.) hail from _____

6.) gather _____

7.) distribute _____

8.) notable _____

9.) familiar _____

10.)essential _____

11.) subscribe _____

12.)forum _____

13.)reddit _____

14.)blog _____

15.)promote a product _____

16.)conference _____

17.) festival _____

18.)trade fair _____

19.) innovation _____

20.)access _____

Answer these questions in complete sentences.

1.) From where do journalists obtain their information?

_____

_____

2.) From which sources does their information mainly come from?

_____

_____

3.) What does a news agency do?

_____

_____

4.) What are the names of the most well-known news agencies?

_____

_____

5.) What is essential for journalists to do?

_____

_____

6.) Why do some companies put out press releases?

_____

_____

7.) What are important sources of information for journalists?

_____

_____

8.) Which three types of event are mentioned in the article?

_____

_____

9.) Why would science and technology journalists attend a science fair?

_____

_____

10.) Which of the social media sites is mostly access by journalists?

_____

_____

Say if these sentences are true (T) or false (F)

1.) Journalists write stories and news items. _____

2.) Their information never comes from personal contacts. _____

3.) A news agency is always a public organisation. _____

4.) A news agency is never a private organisation. _____

5.) The article mentions four news agencies. _____

6.) PR means press release. _____

Choose *a, b, c* or *d*

1.) A journalist _____ his information from many different sources.

   a.) obtaining   b.) obtain   c.) obtains   d.) to obtain

2.) Journalists should _____ to newspapers and magazines.

   a.) subscribe   b.) subscription   c.) subscribes   d.) subscriber

3.) Companies use _____ to tell the public about the things they are selling.

   a.) Agence France-Press   b.) blogs   c.) the public   d.) PR

4.) Reuters is a _____.

   a.) television   b.) newspaper   c.) magazine   d.) news agency

5.) Conferences, festivals and trade fairs give journalists _____ information.

   a.) very little   b.) a lot of   c.) blog   d.) no

6.) _____ media is used by many journalists.

   a.) Many   b.) Public   c.) Social   d.) Trade

UNIT 4
Sound recordists working in television.

The sound recordist is responsible for recording the highest-possible quality of 'live' sound on location or in a studio, usually in sync with the camera. They must use their experience, equipment, technical expertise, and timing to obtain sound according to the instructions of the director. It is necessary that they read and interpret the script before filming so as to determine its technical requirements and how to achieve these requirements. Then they should plan in detail before the filming, test all technical equipment and decide where to position equipment both on the set and on the actors. They are responsible for all aspects of sound operation including boom operation and sound assistants during production. They have to manage equipment, budgets and interactions with other departments.

To be a sound recordist, you need experience in sound recording, a lot of technical and creative skills, and the ability to think on your feet. You also need a strong knowledge of electronics and a deep understanding of picture sound editing. Sound recordists also need good communicating ability. They have to instruct the sound crew on how to produce the types of sound required.

What do these words and phrases from the text mean? Choose from the following list.

allocation of money and planning how to spend it,   in line with / as someone says,   to be able to invent new things and have new ideas,   a need,   to put something in a certain place, adjusting or making changes in film,   sound or print,   the place where actors act and filming is done,   not recorded / happening now,   to know how to do something,   a part of,   someone whose job it is to put the microphone in the right position,   outside of the studio and in a place where filming is done,   you have done this before / it is not your first time, to find out something,   communication between two or more people,   when two or more things and people move together at the same time and same speed,   a piece of paper with writing on it,   to have a lot of knowledge and ability in something,   to say what something or someone means

1.) live (pronounced 'lyv')_____

2.) on location _____

3.) in sync _____

4.) expertise _____

5.) according to _____

6.) interpret _____

7.) script _____

8.) determine _____

9.) requirement _____

10.) to position _____

11.) on set _____

12.) boom operator _____

13.) aspect _____

14.) budget _____

15.) interaction _____

16.) experience _____

17.) creative _____

18.) to think on your feet _____

19.) editing _____

20.) ability _____

Answer the following questions in complete sentences.

1.) For what is the sound recordist responsible?

_____

_____

2.) How does he do this?

_____

_____

3.) What must they use?

_____

_____

4.) How do they use this?

_____

_____

5.) What must they do before filming?

_____

_____

6.) Why must they do this?

_____

_____

7.) How should they plan before the filming?

_____

_____

8.) What should they test?

_____

_____

9.) What have they to manage?

_____

_____

10.) What do you need experience in if you wish to be a sound recordist?

_____

_____

Say if these sentences are true (T) or false (F)

1.) Sound recordists need to interpret a script _____

2.) Sound equipment must be put on the set and on actors. _____

3.) Sound recordists are not responsible for all aspects of sound. _____

4.) They do not have to manage equipment. _____

5.) They have to interact with other departments. _____

6.) They need to have knowledge of electronics. _____

Choose *a, b, c* or *d*

1.) The sound recordist records _____sound.

    a.) dead   b.) live   c.) script   d.) interpret

2.) He does this _____with the camera.

    a.) technical   b.) experience   c.) out of sync   d.) in sync

3.) To be a sound recordist you need _____in sound recording.

    a.) experience   b.) electronics   c.) departments   d.) interact

4.) A sound recordist needs to think _____.

    a.) on his hands   b.) on his head   c.) on his feet
    d.) on his chair

5.) Sound recordists have to _____well.

    a.) communication   b.) communicate   c.) communicates
    d.) communicator

6.) The sound crew _____the types of sound required.

    a.) producing   b.) producer   c.) producers   d.) produces

UNIT 5

On May 27, 1941, the British navy sank the German battleship (whose name was *Bismarck)* in the North Atlantic near France. The German death toll was more than 2,000.

FRANCIS A. ANDREW

On February 14, 1939, the 823-foot *Bismarck* was launched at Hamburg. After the outbreak of war, Britain closely guarded ocean routes from Germany to the Atlantic Ocean, and only U-boats moved freely through the war zone.

In May 1941, the order was given for the *Bismarck* to break out into the Atlantic. Once in the safety of the open ocean, the battleship would be almost impossible to track down, all the while wreaking havoc on Allied convoys to Britain. Learning of its movement, Britain sent almost the entire British Home Fleet in pursuit.

On May 26, the ship was sighted and crippled by British aircraft, and on May 27 three British warships descended on the *Bismarck*, inflicting heavy damage. By mid-morning, the pride of the German navy had become a floating wreck with numerous fires aboard, unable to steer and with her guns almost useless because she was listing badly to port. Soon, the command went out to scuttle the ship, and the *Bismarck* quickly sank. Of a 2,221-man crew, only 115 survived.

What do these words and phrases from the text mean? Choose from the following list.

the ships of war for a country, to send out a ship to sea for the first time, a lot / very many, causing a great amount of damage, seen / spotted, a ship tilting to one side, to deliberately sink a ship by allowing water to enter its hull, not to die / to continue in existence, a ship for fighting in a war, to free oneself from captivity in a confined space, to go downwards, something or someone now on a ship, when something cannot float and goes down under the water, a large sea, a group of ships sailing together, to cause damage to something or injuries to someone, staying on top of the water / not sinking, order someone to do something, the number of people who have died, German submarines, to chase after, an emotional condition from a feeling of worth about something you are connected to, to drive, the start of a war, countries that fight together against a common enemy, all the ships a country owns,   something so badly damaged it cannot be repaired,   to protect,   to find after a long search,   injured or damaged that someone of something cannot move properly, a way,   a place where there is war,   cannot be used

1.) navy _____

2.) battleship _____

3.) death toll _____

4.) launch a ship _____

5.) outbreak of war _____

6.) guard _____

7.) ocean _____

8.) route _____

9.) U boats _____

10.) war zone _____

11.) break out _____

12.) track down _____

13.) wreaking havoc _____

14.) allied _____

15.) convoy _____

16.) fleet _____

17.) pursuit _____

18.) sighted_____

19.) crippled _____

20.) descend _____

21.) inflict _____

22.) pride _____

23.) floating _____

24.) wreck _____

25.) numerous _____

26.) aboard _____

27.) steer _____

28.) useless _____

29.) listing _____

30.) command _____

31.) scuttle _____

32.) sink /sank (past tense) _____

33.) survive _____

Answer these questions in complete sentences.

1.) On which date was the *Bismarck* sunk?

_____

_____

2.) Where was it sunk?

_____

_____

3.) How many Germans were killed?

_____

_____

4.) How long was the *Bismarck*?

_____

_____

5.) From where was it launched?

_____

_____

6.) Where did the *Bismarck* break out into?

_____

_____

7.) What did the British send in pursuit of the *Bismarck*?

_____

_____

8.) How many British warships descended on the *Bismarck*?

_____

_____

9.) How did the *Bismarck* go to port?

_____

_____

10.) How many Germans survived the sinking of the *Bismarck*?

_____

_____

Say if these sentences are true (T) or false (F)

1.) The American navy sank the *Bismarck*._____

2.) The *Bismarck* was launched in 1938. _____

3.) Britain closely guarded the routes from Germany to the Pacific Ocean. _____

4.) U Boats moved freely through the war zone. _____

5.) In 1941, the *Bismarck* was ordered to go into the Atlantic. _____

6.) Britain did not send almost the entire Home Fleet in pursuit. _____

Choose *a, b, c* or *d*

1.) The battleship would be almost impossible to track _____.

   a.) up   b.) in   c.) down   d.) on

2.) Britain _____of the *Bismarck's* movements.

   a.) learned   b.) learn   c.) learning   d.) learners

3.) The ship _____.

   a.) was sight   b.) was sighting   c.) were sighted
   d.) was sighted

4.) There were _____fires aboard the ship.

   a.) number   b.) numerous   c.) numbers   d.) number

5.) The *Bismarck* _____ sank.

    a.) quick b.) quickly c.) quicks d.) quicker

6.) Only _____ of the crew survived.

    a.) one hundred and fifty b.) one hundred and five
    c.) one hundred and fifty one d.) one hundred and fifteen

READING FOR ENJOYMENT

Petra is situated between the Red Sea and the Dead Sea in Jordan. It has been inhabited since prehistoric times. All the buildings have been made by cutting into the rocks in the area. Petra was inhabited by a people called the Nabateans. During the times of the Greeks, and later of the Romans, Petra became a major caravan centre for the incense of Arabia, the silks of China and the spices of India. It was a crossroads between Arabia, Egypt and Syria-Phoenicia. An ingenious water management system allowed extensive settlement of this arid area during the Nabataean, Roman and Byzantine periods. It is one of the world's richest and largest archaeological sites. It is located in a dominating red sandstone landscape.

The value of Petra is in the vast extent of its elaborate architecture; the high places; the remnant channels and the tunnels and diversion dams. In ancient times, these combined with a vast network of cisterns and reservoirs which controlled and conserved seasonal rains. There was also copper mining in the area.

Regulations and policies developed under the Petra Archaeological Park Operating Plan will cover infrastructure projects undertaken by the PRA including electrification of the Petra Archaeological Park and works associated with water recycling farming projects including tree-planting. They will also cover visitor facilities such as park lighting, tourist trails and restaurants and shops, community recreation areas and businesses, and public events and activities within the park.

Answer the questions in complete sentences.

1.) Where is Petra situated?

_____

_____

2.) How long has it been inhabited?

_____

_____

3.) How have the buildings been made?

_____

_____

4.) Who were the people who inhabited Petra?

_____

_____

5.) For what was Petra a major caravan centre?

_____

_____

6.) What is the value of Petra?

_____

_____

7.) What kind of mining was there in the area?

_____

_____

8.) Which organization is doing the infrastructure projects?

_____

_____

9.) What will be planted?

_____

_____

10.) Where will there be public events and activities?

_____

_____

THEME 22

CAREERS

UNIT 1
How to apply for a job

Your job application is the very first way you present yourself to a potential new employer, and so it is very important that you do it correctly.

A job application is a formal document that sums up your factual education and experience for your potential employer. It contains your personal information for recruiters to review.

Sometimes when you go online to submit your curriculum vitae to a company you are asked to fill out a digital application. At other times, companies will ask you to come in and fill out an application by hand. Often this is done during the interview. Unlike your CV, your job application is a legal document. It's important that the information included is thorough and accurate.

Often, recruiters will include a digital job application as part of a job application package where you are asked to submit additional items like your CV, references and cover letter.

Most people search for their jobs on the internet. It is the easiest way to make contact with employers who are looking for the most suitable employees.

If you start your search with a job search rather than a company search, it is important to apply to research every company you send your application to. If you know anyone who already works for one of those companies, ask them for some information about it.

Next, you should make sure that your resume is up to date. Make sure all the information in it is correct. Employers like well-written job applications.

What do these words and phrases from the text mean? Choose from the following list.

to read,   consider and check,   asking a potential employer for a job,   of the law,   look for something,   show yourself, another word for 'curriculum vitae',   precise / exact,   to write with a pen,   a short letter summarising what is in your CV,   give your papers to the potential employer,   to answer all the questions and provide all the information asked for on a document,   a document giving information on your education and previous work experience,   having all the latest and newest information,   letters from people attesting to your good character and abilities,   to make a summary,   detailed,   an official paper,   to look for information about someone or something,   an abbreviation for curriculum vitae,   right / appropriate,   same as the employer.

1.) job application _____

2.) present yourself _____

3.) formal document _____

4.) recruiter _____

5.) review _____

6.) submit your application _____

7.) curriculum vitae _____

8.) fill out _____

9.) legal _____

10.) thorough _____

11.) accurate _____

12.) references _____

13.) cover letter _____

14.) search _____

15.) suitable _____

16.) research _____

17.) resume _____

18.) CV _____

19.) by hand _____

20.) up to date _____

21.) sum up _____

Answer these questions in complete sentences.

1.) What is the first way that you present yourself to a potential new employer?

_____

_____

2.) What does a job application contain?

_____

_____

3.) Which are the two ways that companies might ask you to fill out an application?

_____

_____

4.) What is the difference between a CV and a job application?

_____

_____

5.) Where do most people search for their jobs?

_____

_____

6.) What should you do if you send your application to every company?

_____

_____

7.) Who should you contact to find out information about a company?

_____

_____

8.) What should be up to date?

_____

_____

9.) What should you make sure about all the information in your CV?

_____

_____

10.) What do employers like?

_____

_____

Say if these sentences are true (T) or false (F).

1.) It is unimportant to do your job application correctly.

_____

2.) A job application is an informal document. _____

3.) Sometimes companies ask you to fill out a digital application. _____

4.) Companies never ask you to fill out an application by hand. _____

5.) The easiest way to contact employers is on the internet.

_____

6.) It is a good idea to ask people you know who work in a company to give you some information about it. _____

Choose *a, b, c* or *d*.

1.) A job applications sums up your _____and _____.

a.) education / jobs   b.) CV / resume   c.) education / experience   d.) experience / CV

2.) There is _____ in a job application.

    a.) jobs b.) personal information c.) no information d.) experience

3.) Hand-written applications are done during the _____.

    a.) interview b.) work c.) job d.) digital

4.) Your CV should be _____.

    a.) out of date b.) dated c.) personal experience d.) up to date

5.) The information in a CV should be _____.

    a.) wrong b.) incorrect c.) correct d.) digital

6.) Employers _____ well-written applications.

    a.) dislike b.) like c.) interview d.) information

UNIT 2
How to write a good CV

Your CV, short for curriculum vitae, is a personal document used to convince prospective employers that you are suitable for the job. It should tell them about you, your professional history and your skills, abilities and achievements.

A CV is required when applying for a job. In addition to your CV, employers may also require a cover letter and a completed application form.

The first part of your CV, positioned at the top of the page, should contain your name, professional title and contact details.

A personal profile, also known as a personal statement, career objective and professional profile, is one of the most important aspects of your CV. It's a short paragraph that sits just underneath your name and contact details giving prospective employers an idea of who you are and what kind of person you are.

Keep your personal statement short, no longer than a few sentences. To make this section look good, you should try to say:

1. Who you are
2. What you can offer the company
3. What your career goals and careers

Your education should be listed in reverse chronological order. Include the name of the educational institutions and the dates you were there. This is followed by the qualifications and grades you achieved.

The next part of your CV contains your employment history. You list your previous jobs, internships and work experience.

List your experience in reverse chronological order as your recent role is the most relevant to the employer.

When you write out your employment details, state your job title, the employer, the dates you worked and a line that summarises the role. Then bullet point your key responsibilities, skills and achievements.

Finally, you can include your hobbies and interests in a CV. However, do not make long lists and only include interests that are relevant to the job.

What do these words and phrases from the text mean? Choose from the following list.

something you are able to do, need, a division of a piece of writing contain two or more sentences, about yourself, time succession – starting from the earliest and coming to the present, put in a place, persuade / make someone believe something, a short description about yourself, things which you are interested in, something you have done successfully, extra / more,   things like certificates / diplomas / degrees, what was directly before now,   giving out information in written or spoken form,   part of a student's studies where they gain experience in a practical working situation,   time going backwards / you write the most recent first and then work backwards to the beginning,   the name of your job in a company,   your address,   email address,   phone number, the last thing / the least furthest back in time,   how you want to develop in your working life,   the exact nature of your job, what you are expected to do in your job, ...,   what you like to do in your spare time,   something you know how to do well,   the name of your job,   school / college / academy / university,   most important,   the level you achieved in an exam or test – A+, A, B etc,   to have something inside it,   has connection to something

1.) personal _____

2.) convince _____

3.) ability _____

4.) achievement _____

5.) require _____

6.) addition _____

7.) positioned _____

8.) contain _____

9.) professional title _____

10.) contact details _____

11.) paragraph _____

12.) statement _____

13.) career objective /career goals _____

14.) chronological order _____

15.) reverse chronological order _____

16.) educational institutions _____

17.) qualifications _____

18.) grades _____

19.) previous _____

20.) internship _____

21.) recent _____

22.) role _____

23.) relevant _____

24.) job title _____

25.) bullet points _____

26.) skill _____

27.) key _____

28.) responsibilities _____

29.) hobby _____

30.) interests _____

31.) personal profile _____

Answer the questions in complete sentences.

1.) What is your CV used for?

2.) What should it tell them about?

3.) When is a CV required?

4.) What else, apart from your CV, might your employers require?

5.) Where should you place your personal profile on your CV?

6.) What two things should be listed in reverse chronological order?

7.) What is 'employment history?'

_____

_____

8.) What job is the most relevant to your employer?

_____

_____

9.) What things should you write out in bullet points in your employment details?

_____

_____

10.) Which kind of interests should you include in your CV?

_____

_____

Say if these sentences are true (T) or false (F)

1.) CV is short for resume. _____

2.) A CV is used to convince your employer about your suitability for the job. _____

3.) Employers do not ask for a cover letter along with your CV. _____

4.) The first part of your CV does not contain contact details. _____

5.) A personal profile can also be called a personal statement. _____

6.) A personal profile should consist of long paragraphs. _____

7.) You should give the dates you attended educational institutions. _____

8.) You cannot include your hobbies in a CV. _____

9.) Your interests should be relevant to the job you are applying for. _____

10.) Make long lists of your hobbies and interests. _____

Choose *a, b, c* or *d*.

1.) Your CV is a _____.

    a.) list of your hobbies   b.) personal document
    c.) job application   d.) statement

2.) A personal statement should say _____.

    a.) what job you want   b.) your hobbies
    c.) your interests   d.) who you are

3.) Your educational history should include _____.

    a.) the grades you received   b.) your cover letter
    c.) long paragraphs   d.) employment history

4.) The _____is included in your employment details.

    a.) qualifications   b.) hobbies   c.) job title
    d.) educational institutions

5.) _____your key responsibilities.

    a.) Chronological   b.) Bullet point   c.) Paragraph
    d.) History

UNIT 3
How to write a cover letter for a job.

A cover letter is a formal letter you send with your CV. Its purpose is to elaborate on the information contained in your CV. Unlike a CV, a cover letter allows you to introduce yourself to the hiring manager. It provides context for your achievements and qualifications, and explains your motivation for joining the company.

Your cover letter should have a heading. This should include your name, phone number, email address, the date, the name of the hiring manager and their professional title, and the name and address of the company to which you are applying for a job.

Begin your letter by greeting the person formally with a title such as Professor, Dr., Mr., Mrs., Miss, Ms. This is followed by the surname of the person and not the first name. If you don't know the name of the person but know they are of the male gender, write 'Dear Sir.' If you don't know the name of the person but you know they are female, write 'Dear Madam.' If you know neither the name nor the gender of the person write 'Dear Sir (or Madam).' If you know the person is female but you don't know their marital status write 'Dear Ms.'

This is followed by a short paragraph about your overall experiences in doing the job. You say that this is the reason you can fit in to the company and contribute to its success. It is not very important to list your past achievements. It is more important to show how you can use these achievements to benefit the company you wish to work in.

Say something you know about the company – for example, some project that they are currently undertaking. Then say that you think it is an exciting project and that you can contribute to its development and success.

The final part of your letter should not say how much you want the job. Rather, focus on how you are looking forward to contributing your talents and skills to the company.

Sign out with 'Yours faithfully.' Underneath this sign your name. Under the signature, type your name.

What do these words and phrases from the text mean? Choose from the following list.

a name / title above a text,   having a knowledge of how to do something very well,   the manager who is responsible for recruiting people for the company,   your name as written by pen,   saying something like 'hello,' 'hi,' 'good morning' to someone,   a piece of work or research,   the interrelated conditions around something,   married / single / widowed / divorced,   your family name,   to give more information / details / embellishments,   something which gives advantages, to successfully be a part of some organisation,   a reason that moves you to do something,   when things progress and get better,   to write your signature,   doing a set piece of work, general,   now,   sex – male or female,   give something

1.) elaborate on _____

2.) context _____

3.) motivation _____

4.) heading _____

5.) hiring manager _____

6.) greeting _____

7.) surname _____

8.) gender _____

9.) marital status _____

10.) overall _____

11.) fit in _____

12.) contribute _____

13.) benefit _____

14.) project _____

15.) development _____

16.) undertaking _____

17.) currently _____

18.) talent _____

19.) sign _____

20.) signature _____

Answer these questions in complete sentences.

1.) What is a cover letter?

_____

_____

2.) What is the purpose of a cover letter?

_____

_____

3.) What does it provide?

_____

_____

4.) What does it explain?

_____

_____

5.) What information should your covering letter heading contain?

_____

_____

6.) What name do you use for the person you are writing to?

_____

_____

7.) What is not very important to list?

_____

_____

8.) What is important to say about your previous achievements?

_____

_____

9.) How do you sign yourself out of the letter?

_____

_____

10.) What do you type under your signature?

_____

_____

Say if these sentences are true (T) or false (F)

1.) The cover letter allows you to introduce yourself to the hiring manager. _____

2.) It does not provide a context for your achievements and qualifications. _____

3.) Your cover letter shouldn't have a heading. _____

4.) Use titles like Mr. and Mrs. To start your letter.

5.) If you don't know the name or gender of the person you are writing to, write 'Dear Sir.' _____

6.) Type you name under your signature. _____

Choose *a, b, c* or *d.*

1.) The title of the person you are writing to should be followed by that person's _____.

   a.) first name   b.) Mr.   c.) telephone number   d.) surname

2.) If you know the person you are writing to is a man but you don't know his name, write _____.

   a.) Dear Madam   b.) Dear Sir   c.) Dear Sir (or Madam)
   d.) Dear Manager

3.) You know the name of a woman you are writing to but you don't know if she is married or single. You should address her as _____

   a.) Dear Mrs.   b.) Dear Miss   c.) Dear Ms   d.) Dear Dr.

4.) After the greeting, you write about your job _____.

   a.) interview   b.) needs   c.) experiences   d.) cover letter

5.) You write about your past achievements so as to _____ the company.

    a.) benefit   b.) cover   c.) write to   d.) interview

6.) You say how much you want to contribute your skills and talents to the company in the _____part of your letter.

    a.) first   b.) middle   c.) heading   d.) final

UNIT 4
How to be successful at an interview

A successful interview depends on various factors. It depends on how you prepare and on how you conduct yourself in the meeting. You may have multiple rounds of interviews before receiving a job offer, so it's important to ensure you do the right thing at each one. Regardless of the type of interview you're expecting, you can follow some general guidelines that will help improve your chances of impressing a potential employer. Here in this text, we will provide some tips that can help you achieve success in your interview.

Behaviour-based interviewing is when your interviewer asks you about how you handled past situations at work. This interviewing technique gives a potential employer valuable insight into the way you approach challenges in your job and turn them into favorable opportunities.

You can prepare for this type of interview by making a list of your skills, strengths and weaknesses.

Here are some questions you may be asked at the interview. They are given in bullet points.

- Can you tell me about yourself?
- How did you hear about this job?
- Why do you want this job?
- Why should we hire you?

- What are your strengths?
- What are your weaknesses?
- What do you know about the company?
- Where do you see yourself in five years?
- What is your work ethic?
- What kind of environment do you prefer to work in?
- How do you handle work-related disagreements with your colleagues?
- How would your current employer and colleagues describe you?
- How do you handle pressure?
- Do you have any questions for me?

Always dress smartly before the interview. Do not wear casual clothes like jeans and a T-shirt. The following is a list of things you should bring with you for a successful interview:

- A printed copy of your resume
- A list of references
- Work samples and publications to show the employer
- A list of questions to ask the employer
- A notebook and pen to take notes

What do these words and phrases from the text mean? Choose from the following list.

It doesn't matter / not important one way or the other, to see clearly into a situation, make sure about something, short phrases to help you remember things, of great worth, a list of things to help you do things properly, something that contributes to producing a result, your moral and principled position of how you deal with your work, a small pad for writing down your notes in, many, things that happen, behaviour, difficult situations piling up on top of someone, to make someone see you in a very positive way, make something or someone better, how you deal with someone or something, a method / a way of doing something, when a number of persons do not have the same ideas or opinions about something,

opportunities,   what you like best,   dealing with something /
manipulating it,   documents written by people attesting to your
character,   a difficulty,   short pieces of advice,   someone
who works with you,   the type of place and surroundings of
where you work,   that produce good things / benefits

1.) factor _____

2.) conduct _____

3.) multiple _____

4.) ensure _____

5.) regardless _____

6.) guidelines _____

7.) improve _____

8.) chances _____

9.) impress _____

10.) tips _____

11.) handle _____

12.) situations _____

13.) technique _____

14.) valuable _____

15.) insight _____

16.) approach _____

17.) challenge _____

18.) favourable _____

19.) work ethic _____

20.)work environment _____

21.) prefer _____

22.)disagreement _____

23.)colleague _____

24.)pressure _____

25.)references _____

26.)notebook _____

27.) notes _____

Answer the following questions in complete sentences.

1.) What does a successful interview depend on?

_____

_____

2.) What may you have before receiving a job offer?

_____

_____

3.) What is important to ensure?

_____

_____

4.) What will following general guidelines improve?

_____

_____

5.) What is behaviour-based interviewing?

_____

_____

6.) What does this type of interviewing give potential employers?

_____

_____

7.) How can you prepare for this type of interviewing?

_____

_____

8.) How should you dress before the interview?

_____

_____

9.) Which kind of clothes should you not wear?

_____

_____

10.) What items should you bring to the interview?

_____

_____

Say if these sentences are true (T) or false (F)

1.) How you conduct yourself at an interview is not important.

_____

2.) How you prepare for the meeting is unimportant. _____

3.) The above text gives some tips on how to be successful in an interview. _____

4.) Sometimes the employer asks an interviewee about himself. _____

5.) The interviewer never asks the interviewee about how he would handle pressure. _____

Choose *a, b, c* or *d*

1.) The interviewee should always dress _____

   a.) casually   b.) badly   c.) smartly   d.) informally

2.) It is important to do the _____at an interview.

   a.) right thing   b.) wrong thing   c.) informal   d.) casual

3.) The interviewer will ask you about _____.

   a.) himself   b.) herself   c.) myself   d.) yourself

4.) Bring to the interview a printed copy of your _____.

   a.) book   b.) resume   c.) yourself   d.) passport

5.) You should not wear _____.

   a.) formal clothes   b.) a smart suit   c.) clean clothes
   d.) jeans and a T-shirt.

UNIT 5
Your first day at work

Your first day at a new job is often one of the most memorable and eventful. You'll need to meet your new co-workers, make a good impression, get your workspace set up and learn about your new company's rules and culture. A great performance at these tasks can help your subsequent workdays go more smoothly.

Your first day of work sets the tone for your job going forward. On your first day, you'll learn many of the things you need to know to perform your job well. For instance, the first day is typically when you'll first see your work area, learn your specific day-to-day schedule, meet your co-workers, get familiar with different areas of your office or building. Your first day sets the foundation for all of your future interactions at work

Additionally, you may have searched for weeks or months before finding your new job that suits you, so it's important to make the most of the opportunity you now have to move forward in your career. This means that you should make every possible effort to be prepared for your first day of work.

What do these words and phrases from the text mean? Choose from the following list.

colleagues, appropriate / right, easy to remember, the exact place in a building where you work, do the job, communicate and deal with people, letting people see you are good and worthwhile, what comes after, the first part upon which everything else is built, what the dos and donts and other forms of behaviour are in the company, to get the maximum benefit from something, to arrange things in a particular way, many things happening, make the way things will happen and function, same as workspace, to move without difficulty, a timetable, usually / normally, to get to know someone or something

1.) memorable _____

2.) eventful _____

3.) co-workers _____

4.) workspace _____

5.) company culture _____

6.) subsequent _____

7.) smoothly _____

8.) set the tone _____

9.) perform your job _____

10.) typically _____

11.) work area _____

12.) get familiar _____

13.) schedule _____

14.) foundation _____

15.) interactions _____

16.) suit _____

17.) make the most of something _____

18.) make a good impression _____

19.) set up something _____

Answer the following questions in complete sentences.

1.) What can you say about your first day at work?

_____

_____

2.) Who will you meet?

_____

_____

3.) What will a great performance of the tasks on your first day help?

_____

_____

4.) What does your first day at work set?

_____

_____

5.) What will you learn on your first day?

_____

_____

6.) What do you first see?

_____

_____

7.) What specific thing will you learn?

_____

_____

8.) What will you get familiar with?

_____

_____

9.) How long may you have searched before finding your new job?

_____

_____

10.) What should you make the most of?

_____

_____

Say if these sentences are true (T) or false (F)

1.) You will never remember your first day at work _____

2.) You should not make a good impression. _____

3.) It is necessary to get your workplace set up. _____

4.) You don't need to learn about your new company's rules and culture. _____

5.) Your first day is foundational for how you will perform in your job. _____

Choose *a, b, c* or *d*

1.) On your first day at work you meet your _____.

a.) customers   b.) clients   c.) directors   d.) co-workers

2.) A good first day's performance can help you with your _____workdays.

a.) subsequent   b.) work   c.) perform   d.) day

3.) Your first day sets the _____for your job to progress.

a.) time   b.) workdays   c.) tone   d.) days

4.) You should make every possible _____to be prepared for your first day.

a.) subsequent   b.) progress   c.) culture   d.) effort

5.) Your first day is very _____.

    a.) set up   b.) important   c.) effort   d.) prepare

READING FOR ENJOYMENT

The Eiffel Tower is located in Paris, France. It is the most famous structure in Paris. It was completed in 1889. France wanted to show to the world how industrially advanced it was.

Gustav Eiffel was the engineer who designed the structure. Maurice Koechlin and Emile Nouguier were the men who made the drawings for the monument.

The Eiffel Tower is built of iron. Before the Tower was built, iron was never used as a building material. It was used internally usually as support structures. The Eiffel Tower consists of 18,000 pieces of iron. These were forged in Eiffel's factory which was situated on the outskirts of Paris.

It took two years to build the Tower – work being started in 1887. The cost of construction of the Eiffel Tower was almost eight million gold francs. The Tower stands at 1,063 feet (324 metres). It was the tallest building in the world until it was surpassed by the Chrysler Building in New York in 1930.

The structure weighs 10,000 tons and has 108 stories and 1,710 steps. Although the Eiffel Tower is now 132 years old, it is still very modern in its style. Another interesting thing about this building is that it has no purpose. It was built just as a showpiece for French engineering and industry.

Answer these questions in complete sentences.

    1.) Where is the Eiffel Tower?

    _____

    _____

2.) When was it completed?

_____

_____

3.) How long did it take to build?

_____

_____

4.) When was the building of the Tower started?

_____

_____

5.) Who was the engineer who designed the Tower?

_____

_____

6.) Who made the drawings?

_____

_____

7.) What did France want to show the world by building the Eiffel Tower?

_____

_____

8.) How many pieces of iron does the Eiffel Tower consist of?

_____

_____

9.) How much did the Eiffel Tower cost to construct?

_____

_____

10.) How tall is the Tower?

_____

_____

THEME 23

HEALTH

UNIT 1
The importance of vegetables in your diet.

The Harvard School of Public Health recommends people eat a lot of vegetables every day. Vegetables contain lots of vitamins and minerals. These help us gain good health. Many vegetables contain a lot of potassium, and potassium is good for maintaining a good blood pressure level. Perhaps most importantly, vegetables are rich in a particular group of nutrients called antioxidants, which prevent damage to the cells and help prevent heart disease, cancer, Parkinson's disease, atherosclerosis, heart attack and Alzheimer's disease.

Another substantial benefit of vegetables is dietary fibre. Fibre is an important nutrient found only in plant foods. Fibre helps scour bad cholesterol out of your arteries, thus lowering your risk of heart disease. Fibre also keeps your digestive system running smoothly, helps control your blood sugar levels and may help prevent cancer.

Your immune system is very important. When it's strong, it protects your body against dangerous toxins. When it's weak your body cannot fight off viruses and bacteria. A weakened immune system causes skin disorders, delayed wound healing, upper respiratory infections, aging and chronic illness. Eating more vegetables as part of a healthy diet is an important key to help boost immune health.

What do these words and phrases from the text mean? Choose from the following list.

make bigger / better,   a disease of the brain which causes memory loss,   something that destroys bad things in your body,   advise,   thread-like parts that form plant material, very serious,   the smallest and most basic part of a plant of animal,   a dangerous thing that enters the human body and causes disease,   a network of processes that protects a person from diseases,   an uncontrolled division of the cells of the body, an organic molecule,   a microscopic infectious particle, getting older,   a single-celled organism that causes disease, an illness,   a large amount,   keep something from changing, stop something from happening,   an infection of the nose, sinuses,   pharynx or larynx,   danger,   a substance used by a living thing to grow and reproduce,   clean something thoroughly,   a hurt / damage to a part of the human body,   a hardening of the arteries,   an inorganic solid,   something out of order / not functioning properly,   blood vessels that deliver blood to the heart,   how hard the blood has to push its way through the arteries,   to get something,   a nervous system disease that affects movement,   when the body gets better from a sickness,   a fatty wax-like substance in the cells of the body

1.) recommend _____

2.) vitamin _____

3.) mineral _____

4.) gain _____

5.) potassium _____

6.) maintain _____

7.) blood pressure _____

8.) nutrient _____

9.) antioxidant _____

10.) prevent _____

11.) cell _____

12.)cancer _____

13.)disease _____

14.)Parkinson's disease _____

15.)atherosclerosis _____

16.)Alzheimer's disease _____

17.) substantial _____

18.)fiber _____

19.)cholesterol _____

20.)artery _____

21.)risk _____

22.)toxin _____

23.)virus _____

24.)bacteria _____

25.)disorder _____

26.)wound _____

27.)heal _____

28.)upper respiratory infections _____

29.)aging _____

30.)chronic _____

31.) boost _____

32.)scour _____

33.) immune system _____

Answer these questions in complete sentences.

1.) Which institution thinks people should each vegetables daily?

_____

_____

2.) What do vegetables contain?

_____

_____

3.) What do they help us do?

_____

_____

4.) What can potassium do?

_____

_____

5.) What do antioxidants prevent?

_____

_____

6.) Where is fibre found?

_____

_____

7.) What does fibre do?

_____

_____

8.) What does fibre control?

_____

_____

9.) What does your immune system protect your body from?

_____

_____

10.) What is an important key to boosting your immune health?

_____

_____

Say if these sentences are true (T) or false (F)

1.) There are not many vitamins and minerals in vegetables.
_____

2.) The Harvard School of public Health advises against eating vegetables daily. _____

3.) Antioxidants are nutrients. _____

4.) Antioxidants can prevent Parkinson's disease. _____

5.) Upper respiratory infections are caused by a weakened immune system. _____

Choose *a, b, c* or *d*

1.) Vegetables are _____ in antioxidants.

    a.) poor   b.) immune   c.) rich   d.)system

2.) Vegetables _____ your risk of heart disease.

    a.) lower   b.) heighten   c.) increase   d.) worsen

3.) Vegetables are a source of _____ fibre.

    a.) key   b.) dietary   c.) health   d.) heart

4.) Skin disorders are caused by a _____ immune system.

    a.) strong   b.) good   c.) healthy   d.) weakened

5.) Fibre keeps your digestive system running _____.

    a.) smoothly   b.) slowly   c.) risk   d.) poorly

UNIT 2
The importance of fruit in your diet

Fruits are a good source of vitamins and minerals, recognized for their role in preventing vitamin C and vitamin A deficiencies. People who incorporate fruits and vegetables as part of a healthy eating pattern have a reduced risk of some chronic diseases. Some nutritionists encourage filling half of the plate with fruits and vegetables at mealtimes.

Fruits are an important part of a healthy eating pattern and the source of many vital nutrients, including potassium, folate (folic acid), and antioxidants including polyphenols. Fruit such as blueberries, cranberries, strawberries and citrus also contain phytochemicals which provided added health benefits.

The nutrients in fruit are vital for overall health and maintenance of the body. The benefits of these nutrients include:

- **Reduced risk of chronic disease**: Eating a diet rich in fruit may reduce risk for stroke, cardiovascular disease and type 2 diabetes.
- **Improved heart health**: The potassium in fruit can reduce the risk of heart disease and stroke. Potassium may also reduce the risk of developing kidney stones and help to decrease bone loss.
- **Lower risk of neural tube defects**: Folate (folic acid) helps the body form red blood cells. Women of childbearing age who may become pregnant and those in the first trimester of pregnancy need adequate folate. Folate helps prevent neural tube birth defects such as spina bifida.
- **Protection against cell damage**: An eating pattern where fruit is part of an overall healthy diet provides antioxidants that help repair damage done by free radicals and may protect against certain cancers. It may also have a positive impact on digestive health. Polyphenols are antioxidants that have been shown to alter gut micro-ecology, or the proportion of healthy versus harmful bacteria.

What do these words and phrases from the text mean? Choose from the following list.

a strong effect, job / task, a component of blood that carries oxygen from the lungs to other parts of the body, very tiny, when the body doesn't respond to insulin, to put the maximum amount of things into a container, weeks 1 – 12 of pregnancy, the shape and design of something, when the spine and spinal cord do not form properly, when the body cannot produce insulin, change, disease of the heart, a connection between the brain and the spinal cord for babies in the womb of their mother, the hard parts of which the human skeleton is composed, when blood is cut off to the brain, make something part of another thing, compounds that are produced by plants, unstable molecules that can damage the body, not enough of something,   a solid piece of material that develops in the urinary tract,   a very small system of living organisms, enough,   the relationship of parts to the whole,   persuade, the age at which women can have children,   when food is broken down by the body into its various nutrients,   a scientist who is an expert in what we should and should not eat,   a fault / a flaw,   extremely important,   the spacing and patters of living things,   when a woman is carrying a baby in her womb, part of the digestive tract,   against / opposed to

1.) role _____

2.) deficiency _____

3.) incorporate _____

4.) nutritionist _____

5.) encourage _____

6.) fill _____

7.) pattern _____

8.) vital _____

9.) stroke _____

10.) cardiovascular disease _____

11.) type 1 diabetes _____

12.) type 2 diabetes _____

13.) kidney stones _____

14.) bone _____

15.) red blood cells _____

16.) childbearing age _____

17.) pregnant _____

18.) first trimester of pregnancy _____

19.) adequate _____

20.) neural tube _____

21.) spina bifida _____

22.) defect _____

23.) free radicals _____

24.) digestion _____

25.) alter _____

26.) gut _____

27.) micro _____

28.) ecology _____

29.) micro-ecology _____

30.) proportion _____

31.) versus _____

32.) impact _____

33.) phytochemicals _____

Answer these questions in complete sentences.

1.) What are fruits a good source of?

_____

_____

2.) Which vitamins to they prevent from deficiency?

_____

_____

3.) What do people who eat fruits in their diet have a decreased risk from?

_____

_____

4.) What are polyphenols?

_____

_____

5.) Which fruits contain phytochemicals?

_____

_____

6.) Which three chronic diseases might eating fruit reduce the risk of having?

_____

_____

7.) What is in fruit that can reduce the risk of heart disease and stroke?

_____

_____

8.) What helps the body form red blood cells?

_____

_____

9.) What kind of women need folic acid in their diet?

_____

_____

10.) What do antioxidants do?

_____

_____

Say if these sentences are true (T) or false (F)

1.) Some nutritionists say that you should fill one half of your plate with vegetables and the other half of your plate with fruit at mealtimes. _____

2.) Fruits have many vital nutrients. _____

3.) Phytochemicals give additional health benefits. _____

4.) fruits are inessential for body maintenance. _____

5.) Fruit has no benefits. _____

Choose *a, b, c* or *d*

1.) Type 2 diabetes is a _____ disease.

a.) non   b.) chronic   c.) good   d.) beneficial

2.) _____ contain phytochemicals.

a.) apples   b.) oranges   c.) bananas   d.) blueberries

3.) Folate helps _____ neural birth defects.

    a.) prevents   b.) helps   c.) causes   d.) increases

4.) Free radicals cause _____ to the cells.

    a.) diabetes   b.) folic   c.) damage   d.) benefits

5.) Polyphenols _____ gut micro-ecology.

    a.) neural   b.) pregnant   c.) birth   d.) alter

UNIT 3
The importance of fish in our diet

Fish is packed with many nutrients that most people are lacking. This includes high-quality protein, iodine and various vitamins and minerals.

Fatty species are sometimes considered the healthiest. That's because fatty fish, including salmon, trout, sardines, tuna, and mackerel, are higher in fat-based nutrients.

This includes vitamin D, which many people are lacking.

Fatty fish also has omega 3 fatty acids which are crucial for optimal body and brain function reduce risk of many diseases.

Omega-3 fatty acids are essential for growth and development.

The omega-3 fat is especially important for brain and eye development

For this reason, it's often recommended that pregnant and breastfeeding women eat enough omega-3 fatty acids.

Pregnant women should not eat raw and uncooked fish because it may contain microorganisms that can harm the fetus.

Depression is a common mental condition.

It causes low mood, sadness, and loss of interest in life and activities.

Although it isn't discussed nearly as much as heart disease or obesity, depression is currently one of the world's biggest health problems.

Scientists have found that people who eat fish regularly are much less likely to become depressed.

Numerous experiments also reveal that omega-3 fatty acids may prevent depression and significantly increase the effectiveness of antidepressant medications

Fish and omega-3 fatty acids may also aid other mental conditions, such as bipolar disorder.

What do these words and phrases from the text mean? Choose from the following list.

biomolecules with long chains of amino acids, *overweight / very fat,* *a chemical element,* *a mental condition where a patient has alternative high and low moods,* *very full / full to capacity,* *medicines to treat depression,* *a scientific procedure to discover results,* *types of animals,* *many,* *women feeding their babies with their own breast milk,* *insufficient / not enough of something,* *help,* *think about,* *often,* *how something works,* *concerning things connected to the mind,* *essential / important / vital,* *the best / the highest / to the greatest extent,* *to show something that had not been seen before,* *a baby forming in the womb of its mother,* *meaningful,* *a tiny living thing that can only be seen through a microscope,* *probable*

1.) packed_____

2.) lack _____

3.) protein _____

4.) iodine _____

5.) species _____

6.) consider _____

7.) crucial _____

8.) optimal _____

9.) function _____

10.) breastfeeding _____

11.) mental _____

12.) microorganism _____

13.) fetus _____

14.) obesity _____

15.) likely _____

16.) regularly _____

17.) numerous _____

18.) experiment _____

19.) reveal _____

20.) significant _____

21.) antidepressant medications _____

22.) aid _____

23.) bipolar disorder _____

Answer these questions in complete sentences.

1.) What is fish packed with?

_____

_____

2.) Which fish species are considered to be the healthiest?

_____

_____

3.) What are these fish high in?

_____

_____

4.) What is omega 3 essential for?

_____

_____

5.) What is omega 3 especially important for?

_____

_____

6.) What is one of the world's biggest health problems?

_____

_____

7.) Which kind of people are less likely to become depressed?

_____

_____

8.) What may omega 3 fatty acids prevent?

_____

_____

9.) What may omega 3 fatty acids increase the effectiveness of?

_____

_____

10.) What other mental condition may omega 3 help?

_____

_____

Say if these sentences are true (T) or false (F)

1.) Many people have enough of the nutrient fish is packed with. _____

2.) Fish does not contain high quality protein _____

3.) Sardines are not fatty fish. _____

4.) Tuna is a fatty fish. _____

5.) Pregnant women should eat omega 3 fatty acids. _____

Choose *a, b, c* or *d*

1.) Iodine is a _____

    a.) nutrient b.) fatty acid c.) omega 3 d.) fish

2.) Fatty species of fish are the _____.

    a.) healthy b.) healthier c.) health d.) healthiest

3.) Depression is a _____illness.

a.) stomach   b.) considered   c.) mental   d.) recommended

4.) Raw and uncooked fish may contain _____ which are harmful.

a.)   nutrients   b.)   vitamins   c.)   omega   3   d.) microorganisms

5.) Fish can help people with bipolar _____.

a.) order   b.) disorder   c.) omega   d.) mental

UNIT 4
The importance of nuts in our diet

New evidence has shown that eating too few nuts and seeds gives you an increased risk of dying from cardiovascular disease or diabetes.

One drawback to nuts is that they're high in calories, so it's important to limit portions. But choosing nuts instead of a less healthy snack may keep your heart healthy.

Researchers have found that people who are at risk of a heart attack can cut their risk by eating a healthy diet that includes nuts.

Research suggests that eating nuts may:

- Lower your low-density lipoprotein (LDL or "bad") cholesterol and triglyceride levels, which play a major role in the buildup of deposits called plaques in your arteries
- Improve the health of your arteries
- Lower levels of inflammation that cause heart disease
- Reduce the risk of developing blood clots, which can lead to a heart attack and death

As a result, nuts can improve your heart health and lower your risk of dying early from heart disease and other causes.

Besides being packed with protein, most nuts contain at least some of these heart-healthy substances:

- **Unsaturated fats.** It's not entirely clear why, but it's thought that the "good" fats in nuts — both monounsaturated and polyunsaturated fats — lower bad cholesterol levels.
- **Vitamin E.** Vitamin E may help stop the development of plaques in your arteries, which can narrow them. Plaque development in your arteries can lead to chest pain, coronary artery disease or a heart attack.

Nut oils also are a good source of healthy nutrients, but they lack the fiber found in whole nuts. Walnut oil is the highest in omega-3s.

What do these words and phrases in the text mean? Choose from the following list.

sore, information that indicates the truth about something, disadvantage, the response of the body to damage caused to it, an amount, reduce the danger of, a type of fruit composed of a hard shell, to put down and to remain there, an embryonic plant enclosed in a protective outer covering, the part of your body below your throat and above the stomach, a unit of energy obtained from food, say, someone who looks for information, a clump of blood that has changed from a liquid to a gel, a small meal between main meals

1.) evidence _____

2.) nuts _____

3.) seeds _____

4.) drawback _____

5.) calorie _____

6.) portion _____

7.) snack _____

8.) researcher _____

9.) cut risk _____

10.) suggest _____

11.) deposit _____

12.) inflammation _____

13.) blood clot _____

14.) chest _____

15.) pain _____

Answer the following questions in complete sentences.

1.) What has new evidence shown?

_____

_____

2.) What is one drawback?

_____

_____

3.) What is it important to do?

_____

_____

4.) How might you keep your heart healthy?

_____

_____

5.) How can people who are at risk of heart attack cut their risk?

_____

_____

6.) What is LDL?

_____

_____

7.) What does inflammation cause?

_____

_____

8.) What can blood clots do?

_____

_____

9.) What are nuts packed with?

_____

_____

10.) What are the names of the two types of fats in nuts?

_____

_____

Say in these sentences are true (T) or false (F)

1.) 1) Eating nuts and seeds increases your risk of heart disease. _____

2.) Cholesterol can cause plaque in your arteries. _____

3.) Nuts do not improve the health of your arteries. _____

4.) Vitamin E causes the development of plaques in your arteries. _____

5.) Plaque causes pain in the stomach. _____

Choose *a, b, c* or *d*

1.) _____fats lower cholesterol levels.

a.) Bad   b.) Saturated   c.) Triglyceride   d.) Unsaturated

2.) Monounsaturated fats and polyunsaturated fats are _____ fats.

a.) bad   b.) good   c.) LDL   d.) cholesterol

3.) Plaques can _____the arteries.

a.) narrow   b.) widen   c.) close   d.) increase

4.) Nut oils are a good _____of healthy nutrients.

a.) fats   b.) narrow   c.) unsaturated   d.) source

5.) Walnut oil is the _____in omega 3.

a.) high   b.) highest   c.) higher   d.)height

UNIT 5
The importance of water in our diet

Ask any healthy person you know for a quick health tip, and the first thing they will say is: drink more water. Drinking water requires no effort, no exertion and it is simply something our body forces us to consume anyway.

However, while we pay attention to our food, we tend to forget that water forms a part of our regular diet too. We might consume different cuisines, but the one thing that remains constant through all our meals is water. This is because water is absolutely essential to human health. There are various benefits of drinking water.

Water hydrates the body. This is one of the primary benefits of drinking water, and the reason why our body compels us to drink regularly. The human body is dependent on water to process almost all of its daily functions. In fact, a human being can survive longer without food than without water. Our bodies are composed of about 55-60% water, so water also helps in the creation of saliva, the process of blood circulation, maintaining body temperature and the absorption and transportation of nutrients throughout the body.

Drinking water has a direct impact on your metabolism and results in your body immediately experiencing a spike in energy levels. A study has even shown that drinking only half a litre of water can help your metabolism levels to rise by 30 percent. A person can avoid becoming dehydrated by drinking ample amounts of water.

Water can help you lose weight. If you drink more water, you will eat less because you feel less hungry. It also makes you more physically active. And the more exercise and sports you do, the more your body will burn excess fat.

What do these words and phrases from the text mean? Choose from the following list.

plenty, main/ first / most important, hard effort, the movement of the blood around the body, types of food / dishes, a big and sudden increase, staying the same, to be incorporated into something – like water on a sponge, a habit, too much of something, to take into the body, your body changing what you eat and drink into energy, to force someone to do something, when the body loses a large amount of water, a fluid produced in the mouth, when something has water taken into it

1.) exertion _____

2.) consume _____

3.) tend _____

4.) cuisine _____

5.) constant _____

6.) hydrate _____

7.) primary _____

8.) compel _____

9.) saliva _____

10.) blood circulation _____

11.) absorption _____

12.) metabolism _____

13.) spike _____

14.) dehydrated _____

15.) ample _____

16.) excess _____

Answer these questions in complete sentences.

1) What will a healthy person tell you to do?

_____

_____

2.) What does drinking water not require?

_____

_____

3.) What do we tend to forget?

_____

_____

4.) What remains constant throughout all our meals?

_____

_____

5) Why is this?

_____

_____

6) What does water do to the body?

_____

_____

What percentage of our bodies are composed of water?

_____

_____

17.) What can drinking half a litre of water do?

_____

_____

18.) What will you do less of if you drink more water?

_____

_____

19.) What will happen if you do more sports and exercises?

_____

_____

Say if these sentences are true (T) or false (F)

1.) Drinking water is not hard to do. _____

2.) We can survive longer without water than we can without food. _____

3.) Water dehydrates the body. _____

4.) Water does not help with blood circulation. _____

5.) Drinking water helps increase metabolism. _____

Choose *a, b, c* or *d*

1.) Water forms part of our _____ diet.

a.) regular   b.) irregular   c.) metabolism   d.) dehydrated

2.) Water is _____ to human health?

a.) inessential   b.) bad   c.) essential   d.) dehydrated

3.) Water helps in the _____ of saliva.

a.) increase   b.) creation   c.) decrease   d.) regular

4.) Water can help you lose _____.

a.) weigh   b.) weight   c.) weighs   d.) weighing

5.) Water makes a person physically _____.

a.) action   b.) actions   c.) act   d.) active

READING FOR ENJOYMENT
Pizza

Pizza was born in Naples, the city invented it.

It soon became famous all over the world.

Pizza Margherita was certainly born in Naples: the most famous and the simplest of pizzas that with tomato sauce, mozzarella and basil also brings the colors of the Italian flag to the plate.

It is said that Queen Margherita of Savoy, during one of her stays in the city at Villa Rosebery, wanted to try that popular, simple and delicious food that many of her fellow citizens loved.

Brandi's pizza chef in Chiaia made her try the pizza and called it by her name: Margherita.

You cannot take a tour of Italy without tasting a real Neapolitan pizza, perhaps tasted in in famous pizzerias and without the enrichment of too many useless ingredients.

Of course, nowadays there are good and also excellent pizzerias all over the country and often this humble dish becomes an excuse to be a base of excellent dough with ingredients put on it, but the basic consumer pizza, whether Italian or foreign, is basically a choice between soft Neapolitan style pizza or the crispest Roman style pizza.

Other regions offer similar recipes, the best known of which are the Palermo "Sfinciuni" or the recipes of the Italian Riviera where we find Sardenaira in Sanremo or Pisciarà or Pisciadella in Ventimiglia.

But if you want to taste a great and true pizza, it is in Italy that you will have to do it: where we find pizza and similar preparations in Naples, Rome, and Palermo,

Answer the following questions in complete sentences.

1.) Where was pizza born?

_____

_____

2.) What is the simplest of all the pizzas?

_____

_____

3.) What colours are brought to this pizza?

_____

_____

4.) Who is this pizza named after?

_____

_____

5.) What are there all over the country?

_____

_____

6.) What are the two basic choices of pizza?

_____

_____

7.) What are the best known regions for pizza recipes?

_____

_____

8.) Where do you have to go for a real pizza?

_____

_____

9.) Who was the Queen of Savoy?

_____

_____

10.) Which city did she stay at?

_____

_____

Printed in the United States
by Baker & Taylor Publisher Services